REAL LIVES

REAL LIVES

by D.J.CARSWELL

To Dawn
May God bless you to-day!
J Carswell
2003

Authentic
LIFESTYLE

Authentic Lifestyle is an imprint of Authentic Media,
PO Box 300, Carlisle, Cumbria, CA3 0QS, UK
and PO Box 1047, Waynesboro, GA 30830-2047, USA
www.paternoster-publishing.com

British Library Cataloguing in Publication Data

A catalogue record for this book is available from the British
Library
ISBN 1-85078-412-4

Cover design by Diane Bainbridge
Printed in Great Britain by
Cox and Wyman, Reading, Berkshire

Contents

Preface

All my stories are true.

Each person is real and alive today.

You may know one of them; they may have given you this book.

The chapters are arranged so that you can read them in any order, all at once, or occasionally.

Some are short, one is long, and one is my own story.

You may be an atheist or an agnostic, religious or irreligious, or one of the millions who haven't really given God a thought.

Perhaps as you read of the inner thoughts of individuals, from very different backgrounds and from various angles, you may find them helpful in answering the 'Big Questions' . . .

'Is there a God and if so, is He interested in me?'

Introduction

Every time I travel on a busy tube in London I look around and wonder who all these strangers are around me – crowds of people consisting of individuals who are unique and who possess a life story. What are their backgrounds, where are they going, what is their purpose in life?

If you are anything like me and enjoy reading about people, be it the famous, the infamous or the 'ordinary', then I hope you will find my selection of stories interesting.

I have selected just thirteen men and women – their connection being that they also have a faith story. Mostly, I have been introduced to them through my husband's work.

I am deeply grateful to all the contributors for their co-operation and permission, to Hilary Price for editing the manuscript and to Hazel Fenwick for typing it.

Special thanks too to the real people in my own life for allowing me the time to write – my family, Roger, Emma, Ben, Hannah and Jonathan.

1. THE THIEF

Barry Davis

Prison guards escorted Barry to the grossly-over-crowded cells.

The motley crowd of inmates seemed so young, yet many had committed outrageous crimes, including murder. Perhaps the prisoners wondered who on earth this Englishman was, with the build of a boxer, a funny Spanish accent and a never-ending smile?

Fortunately, Barry was only visiting!

His travels had taken him halfway round the world to South America where life was vastly different from his home town in Lancashire, England.

Looking into the faces of those dark-haired young lads – faces hardened by crime and the poor conditions – maybe Barry's mind wandered back to the circumstances leading up to a 'chance' meeting with an Irish family which altered the course of his life.

Barry does not have very many childhood memories. Those he does have are tainted with the painful touch of tragedy. His mother and father had five children: three girls and two boys. Barry was number four and, when he was only seven years old, his mother died of a brain haemorrhage.

'The last time I saw my mother alive was in the lounge at home. When I next saw her, ironically, she was in the same room, but in a coffin,' recalls Barry with sadness.

Barry's dad was only thirty-six years of age at the time.

Although friends of the family worked tirelessly with his sisters to avoid the children being taken into care by the social services, they could not prevent Barry getting into trouble.

By the age of fifteen, Barry was already dealing in stolen goods. A Saturday job with a lorry business introduced him to a world which revolved around money: a lifestyle which was unknown to him before. He began to steal to keep in with the friends he had made in the local pub, where he was a regular. In the last year of school, Barry's life took a turn for the worse. He began to fight with his dad, was expelled from school and his police record began to grow. Consequently, he was sent to a detention centre for what was called the 'short, sharp shock' treatment. Once the six weeks were up, he emerged, still having an uncontrollable temper and a persistent problem with stealing. The only difference was that he was simply a little more cautious.

In an attempt to control his temper, Barry took up boxing. This was a mixed blessing as it involved associating with some very shady characters. Barry seemed to be on an uncontrollable downward spiral, despite attempts to salvage his troubled life.

A job with a construction company meant he had money in his pocket. In fact, he even managed to buy a house. He began to acquire possessions. Soon, the love of money and `things' began to entwine and strangle his life again.

In May 1987, Barry began working with an Irish Catholic man who had twelve children! Although he was not aware of this at first, this was to be a turning point in Barry's life. As Barry worked alongside his mate, he discovered, from conversations, that several of the twelve children had become 'born-again' Christians. Barry's previous experience of this type of person was limited to recollections of The Daily Mirror newspaper reports on the visit to Blackpool by the American evangelist Billy Graham.

To be quite frank, Barry didn't have much interest in God.

To him, God was something you found out about when you died. It wasn't that he didn't believe in God, but he didn't understand how you could know God in a real way – being a Christian meant just attending church in smart clothes on Sundays and that sort of thing!

Slowly, Barry got to know some of the children who were Christians. He remembers one girl in particular. She lived in Leeds, was a physiotherapist and owned her own house. Her dad used to take Barry along with him when he visited her to do odd jobs around the house.

'The very first time I met her I could tell that there was something different about her. I couldn't explain it.'

She introduced him to her friends. He studied closely how they behaved - and was impressed! They never preached at him, but he was intrigued.

His mind went back to his early childhood when his mother had been alive.

'. . . she had sent us, holding hands in a line, up the cobbled streets to the local Baptist Mission hall, to Sunday School. I only attended for about two years,' remembers Barry.

His lifestyle since those days was a far cry from those times of childhood innocence.

A poster, on the back of one of the doors in Philomena's house, caught Barry's eye. It was the famous poem about footprints:

FOOTPRINTS IN THE SAND

One night a man had a dream.
He dreamed he was walking along the beach with the Lord.
Across the sky flashed scenes from his life.
For each scene, he noticed two sets of footprints in the sand:
One belonging to him, and the other to the Lord.
When the last scene of his life flashed before him,
He looked back at the footprints in the sand.
He noticed that many times along the path of his life
There was only one set of footprints.
He also noticed that it happened
At the very lowest and saddest times in his life.
This really bothered him and he questioned the Lord about it.
'Lord, you said that once I decided to follow you,
You'd walk with me all the way.
But I have noticed that during the most troublesome times in my life
There is only one set of footprints.
I don't understand why when I needed you most, you would leave me.'
The Lord replied, 'My precious, precious child,
I love you and I would never leave you.
During your times of trial and suffering,
When you see only one set of footprints in the sand
It was then that I carried you.'

                                                            Anon

'By this time I was getting interested in the kind of Christianity I had seen being lived out in the lives of Philomena, her brother, Vinny and other 'saved' members of her family.

I would ask lots of questions. The gospel message was explained to me. I don't think I had ever heard it before. Someone told me his story of how he had become a Christian, how sin separates us from God, but Jesus had died to bridge that gap to bring us back to God. I really didn't understand it at all.' Barry remembers thinking, 'It can't be that simple . . . so easy . . .

'A man gave me a Bible to read. He told me to read it for myself and see what God had done and why Jesus had died for me personally. I had never been bothered with books, but I started to get interested in this one. I had read most of the New Testament when I came to realise who Jesus Christ was, why He had died, and that He was alive and could change my life. There was a lot I didn't understand, but I understood enough to ask God to save me and change me.'

As Barry read the Bible, he realised that if he became a Christian his life would change. Some of the company he kept and things he did would have to be different. He thought seriously about the cost of becoming a Christian.

One day soon after this, he came to a point when, through what he had read and through the working of God in his life, he knew he had to act upon what he had learned. He had to accept it and trust Christ as his Lord and Saviour or do nothing and reject all that God had shown him.

'I saw that all the things that were stopping me becoming a Christian were nothing compared to the benefits of trusting Jesus. I took the step of committing my life to Christ. I got on my knees and asked God, if He was there, to come into my life and change me.

'That prayer was the first one I can remember praying seriously in my life; I have not been the same since.'

Barry knew that God had answered his prayer that night. He experienced a peace within which he had never known before. He received the same joy that he had seen in the Christians he had met. He stopped swearing and over a period of time many other things changed, including his bad temper and stealing habits. Also, God gave him a desire to read the Bible and pray. He felt he had entered a relationship in life, which he had never known existed.

Since he became a Christian, things haven't always been easy for Barry. Some people thought that it was just another of his schemes; others thought that he had gone mad; some said it wouldn't last.

God doesn't promise a cosy life, but He does promise that He will never leave us (Heb. 13:5).

'I realise that becoming a Christian was the best and most important decision I had ever made in my life. I have the confidence of knowing that my sins are forgiven and that I have a place in heaven. I don't deserve any of this. I only have this assurance because I am trusting in what Jesus has done for me.'

Barry Davis went on to study at Belfast Bible College. For several years he worked in a rehabilitation centre for prisoners. After a short trip to South America, he felt that God was calling him to work there full-time. He now lives in Nicaragua, sharing the gospel with prisoners in the jails of that country. He is married to Soosun and they have one child.

If you are a prisoner, ex-offender or family member of the former and would like help with any spiritual questions, please contact:

The Prison Fellowship, PO Box 945, Malden,
CM9 4EW

Or: Day One, No 3 Epsom Business Park, Kiln Lane,
Epsom, KT17 1JGF

Further reading: Born Again by Chuck Colson –
ISBN 0-35063-058-2, Hodder

2. THE HOLY MAN

Bhaskar Rao

The young man grabbed a few bananas from the table, before rushing out into the street. The fruit was not, however, to satisfy the hunger in his stomach, but rather, to appease the Hindu god in the temple, where he was heading.

Breathless, he arrived with his gift.

Bowing low, he carefully placed the fruit at the feet of the garish god.

Would it be pleased with the offering? Bhaskar Rao wondered. Would it keep harm away from his family?

He hoped so – but couldn't be sure.

The enormous, inanimate statue made of stone was brightly coloured and hideous to look at. The decorations, emphasising sexual parts, were both intricate and elaborate. Fear, superstition and uncertainty filled the air, as did the sweet, sickly incense burned to find favour with this particular god. (There are thousands of Hindu gods.)

Bhaskar Rao, for that was the name of the young man, was born into a high caste Brahmin family in Andra Pradesh, India. He was the eldest, having four brothers and two sisters. For him, life was strewn with great privileges and status, unlike the lives of thousands of other people born into a lower caste. As far as his religion was concerned, he was extremely devout. To be a good Hindu entailed being well behaved, reading religious scriptures, meditation and chanting the names of gods, visiting temples and going on pilgrimages. This was no problem for him as he was extremely happy to be involved and to comply with everything.

'My religion taught me that sooner or later I was going to die, and that once I had died, I would go through the process of reincarnation. Even after following all the traditions, the answer to the question, "Is there any assurance of eternal life?" was always, "No."

'There was turmoil going on in my life, in spite of the fact that I felt that no one could pinpoint any fault in my life at all. I was trying to break from the cycle of transmigration or reincarnation. I didn't want to come back as a cat or pig or monkey.'

Two things in particular had made Bhaskar Rao feel totally dissatisfied and frustrated.

His grandfather was the most religious person he had ever met on the face of the earth. Yet, when the old man was dying, he made it very plain to his grandson that in front of him he saw the angels of death, who were taking him to hell. Bhaskar found this incredibly frustrating because, as a little boy, he used to see his grandfather worshipping for two hours every day before he had a cup of coffee.

'He knew the religious scriptures by heart. He was one of the most religious people, but he died knowing full well that he was going to hell and that terrified me!'

The other thing that disturbed Bhaskar Rao was the sudden death of his uncle, who was just six years older than him; in fact, they were more like brothers. He died in the middle of the night and it was such a shock. His ashes were taken to the river Ganges, because Hindus believe that if your ashes are thrown into the river, you will probably get a better incarnation the next time.

Six months later, when their cow gave birth, it was the combined belief of all the family that the calf was the reincarnation of the uncle. This absolutely shattered Bhaskar Rao. He was only sixteen years old, but was utterly frustrated by the inability of anyone to answer the many questions about a man's final destiny that filled his mind.

Such frustrations only led him to become even more of a religious fanatic. It finally came to the point where he was on the verge of accepting that his role was to go to the Himalayas to vow to become a religious man, who would spend most of his life in meditation.

This would mean quite a change in circumstances for him. For one thing, it would be very cold there! Bhaskar wasn't too sure how he would cope. His home life and caste position meant that he did not lack anything materially or in love. He was not poor, far from it; there was nothing he could want for.

One Saturday, while at university, he was feeling particularly frustrated with life. He wasn't searching for answers in any other religion, he was only doing what his own would have him to do. The realisation that sooner or later, death would come to him with the prospect of reincarnation, led him, that day, to pray to gods and goddesses.

'Normally when we pray, it is by chanting or meditation, offering flowers and incense. This day I said to the gods and goddesses, that I had in front of me, "I would like to worship you today, not with anything else but my own blood".'

Priests never sacrifice animals or humans in the Hindu system of worship. However, that day, Bhaskar was so dispirited within himself that he thought he would offer up his own blood. Taking a pin, he pricked his thumb until sticky red drops of blood appeared, which he smeared all over the pictures of gods in front of him.

With sincerity, he asked the gods, 'Tell me tonight how I can come to you. Any sacrifice you ask of me would not be too great. I am prepared to do anything in return for one thing and one thing alone - I don't need to come back in any form of reincarnation.

'If you don't tell me tonight, tomorrow I am going to commit suicide.'

A look of desperation came over his face. In all seriousness, he really meant to take his own life – although in his heart of hearts, he knew it was a threat to his gods, because he thought that they would be so upset that a great devotee, like him, was going to die.

Saturday night came and went without the gods doing anything.

By Sunday afternoon, Bhaskar was becoming even more desperate.

'I had told lies in my life, so I didn't want to be a liar in this most important thing. Therefore, I prepared a plate of poisoned food that would kill me. I was living alone – there was no one around, so I thought I would lock the door, eat the food and die. After a few days, someone would come and find my decomposed body.'

That was his basic intention. But before he ate his last and fatal meal, he decided to go for a walk along the streets of Madras for one last time. Outside the High Court building, in the centre of the city, an Indian man was giving out leaflets. Bhaskar took one from the man's hand. On the front of the paper it said, 'BLOOD IS NEEDED!'

He asked the gentleman genuinely, 'Is it a blood bank? If it is, you can take as much blood as you want [after all he was about to take his own life, so his blood would not be needed for much longer], but leave me enough to get home to eat my meal! I am prepared to give it. I don't want any money for it.'

'Oh, no it isn't a blood bank,' the Indian politely assured him. 'A group of students and teachers have a meeting, for the public, every Sunday. Do you have time to come along?'

As the only thing on the agenda for that day was suicide, Bhaskar thought that a slight delay would not make any difference. The station, from which he was to catch his train home, was only three minutes away!

Bhaskar followed the man into a room nearby. The people, who had gathered there sang a few songs, which he did not understand. When the Indian stood up to speak, most of what was being said went right over Bhaskar's head!

'Nothing seemed to make sense to me, except for one sentence he kept repeating – "Believe on the Lord Jesus Christ and you will be saved and have eternal life." What caught my attention were the words, "will have." The certainty with which he said those words really hit me. All my life, up until that moment, I had heard people telling me "maybe" or "perhaps." Nothing I tried ever seemed to have any certainty – until this man uttered those powerful words, "will have".'

After the meeting, Bhaskar approached the man who had invited him, and said, 'Sir, who is this man Jesus you keep talking about? I have never heard of him before.' All the incantations of the supreme Hindu gods he knew so well but this incantation he had never heard before.

The man told him that all he could do was to show him something from his religious book, the Bible. He opened it at John's gospel, chapter three and verse sixteen: 'For God so loved the world that He gave His one and only Son, that whoever believes in Him should not perish but will have everlasting life.'

He told Bhaskar to read it again but this time inserting his own name, so it read: ' For God so loved Bhaskar that He gave His one and only Son for Bhaskar that if Bhaskar believes in Him, Bhaskar will not perish, but will have eternal life.'

'It was electrifying!' he says, looking back, savouring those first few moments of understanding. 'To imagine that God loves me so much that He would do all that for me!'

The man then offered to pray for him. Of course, Bhaskar did not really understand what prayer was. Up until that day he had never met a Christian. As they both bowed their heads to pray, Bhaskar experienced the feeling that Someone was near, who removed a huge burden from him, and threw it away. (Years later, he read the book, *Pilgrim's Progress*, by John Bunyan. When he came to the part where the character called Christian comes to the cross and sees his burdens rolling away, Bhaskar exclaimed, 'Oh, that's just what happened to me!')

Bhaskar Rao left the building to catch the train home. He opened the door and saw, lying on the table, his meal of poison. With firm resolve, he threw the food away.

'God, I don't know who you are. I heard about you today and if you can satisfy the desire I have, I am willing to follow You for the rest of my life.'

He was nineteen years old.

Something had happened when he prayed, for he had the assurance that he was forgiven and was certain of eternal life because of what Jesus Christ had done.

'I don't need to be good enough for eternal life, my goodness is my Lord Jesus Christ. He has taken my sinfulness and given me His goodness.'

Bhaskar Rao didn't immediately tell his family what had happened to him. He waited until the moment came when he said publicly, at his baptism, that he had renounced his old life to become a follower of Jesus Christ.(Baptism is like a badge: it doesn't make a person a Christian, but is an identification with the death and resurrection of Jesus Christ.)

The family's immediate reaction was one of anger, resulting in him being thrown out of the home. In their eyes he was considered as dead: one who had gone from them and did not belong anymore.

Although that was very hard for him, he never wavered in his faith.

'I may have lost my religion but I have exchanged it for a relationship with God through Jesus Christ. Religion is man-made – the gospel is God-made. God is the One who wants to make people His own. God has even restored my own family back to me in various ways. The Bible says, "It is appointed unto man once to die and after death, the judgement" (Heb. 9:27) – not eight hundred million, four thousand times!'

If you would care to know more about how you can find the way to God please contact:

BCIEF, 64 Osborne Road, Levenshulme,
Manchester, M19 2DY.

(The utmost confidentiality will be observed)

3. THE DOCTOR

Sally Venn

It was early morning.

The sun was already wide awake and raring to go on its mission to scorch the earth and its inhabitants.

A young Englishwoman tossed back her fair hair, as she prepared for the long day ahead under a hot sun. Looking out from her tiny, concrete room, on the small compound to her left she could see the coconut grove. A lady, draped in a brightly coloured sari, was milking a skinny cow. Beautiful Indian girls were already up and about, sweeping the dusty paths.

The amenities left much to be desired. There was no en-suite bathroom with gold-coloured taps, fluffy towels and bubble bath. Just one cold tap – four hundred yards away. The toilet was a squat loo. If you have never used one before, be thankful! The neighbours were very friendly and made themselves at home – neighbours being mosquitoes, frogs and cockroaches!

Sally thought back over the years, which had brought her from respectable boarding school in Wales, to the beautiful land of India, with the contrasting opulence of the Taj Mahal and the squalor of the vast, over-populated cities.

Surrounded by hundreds of man-made idols of all colours, shapes and sizes, it all seemed a far cry from those early childhood nights back at home in England, when her father would kneel by her bedside to pray with her ...

Sally Venn was privileged to be born into a loving, close family, where moral values were important and were taught in a loving way. Going to church was part of the weekly routine. She had always believed in the God of the Bible, although she sometimes wondered just who He was and what He looked like!

'I knew that He lived in heaven and I suppose I believed that everyone went there unless they were very bad. I knew about Jesus and thought that He was a good man, who taught us the way that we should live.'

Her parents encouraged the three daughters to work hard at school, as they wanted them all to have a good education. But Sally began to struggle a little. She was unhappy and, in consequence, her work suffered. A change of school was decided upon. At the age of twelve, Sally became a boarder and settled in well. Everything was fine, apart from the long weekends, which she found quite boring. It was then that she missed home the most.

Towards the end of her first term, a friend invited her to see the film, *Treasures of the Snow*, which was being shown at one of the meetings organised by a Christian teacher. Sally decided to go, mainly just to fill the time. To her surprise, she was very impressed by the film – so much so, she decided to go to the meeting the following week. This time there was some singing and a serial story that was very much geared for that young age group. A verse from the Bible was also learned, followed by an explanation of the gospel message by the teacher.

'The truth of the simple message hit home to me very powerfully. I understood that Jesus was God in human form and that He died to forgive us our sins.'

Sally had a very tender conscience. She knew that, although she hadn't robbed a bank or done anything outrageously bad, nevertheless, she had done wrong and it was cutting her off from God. Despite being christened, it seemed that just being 'religious', wouldn't enable her to get into heaven.

'I wanted to have a relationship with God – to have the peace and assurance of knowing my sins were forgiven and that I would go to heaven.'

Sally felt she could not live a life worthy of God, and although she wanted to live to follow Christ, she did not trust herself to keep it up.

'I did not want to make promises to God that I would break, so I decided to turn over a new leaf and live as I thought a Christian should, before committing myself properly.'

Of course, this was doomed to fail, as it is not what we do that saves us, but what Christ has already done, by dying on the cross.

One Sunday, the teacher took the class to an old people's home to lead a service. Whilst she was speaking, Sally thought long and hard about what she was hearing. A battle was going on inside her. Did God really exist? Silently, she prayed to God to forgive her. There was no flash of lightning and no one else in the room knew what was happening, but Sally knew that God had answered her prayer. Over the following months and years, her faith began to grow as she learned more about Jesus Christ.

Teenage years could be described as, 'white-water rafting in the river of life!' Sally didn't find them very easy. Pressure mounted as exams loomed on the horizon. Finally, the moment came when she actually achieved her ambition, and went to Bristol University to study medicine.

'I loved university life. I made loads of friends and it was great fun. However, in my quieter moments, I began to feel lonely. I wondered what the point of this socialising was. I knew that the only friend you can rely on is Jesus, but I think my faith had waned a little.'

She started going to church and to some Christian Medical Fellowship meetings, where she met someone who was to change her life – and her name!

Carl was also studying medicine and a committed Christian. In January 1982 at a conference, at which the speaker was George Verwer, of Operation Mobilisation, Sally decided to rededicate her life to her Lord, being willing to go wherever He wanted her to serve. At the same time, she was growing increasingly aware that she was very fond of Carl! So much so that she began to think that this was the man she wanted to spend the rest of her life with.

In October 1982 they became officially engaged – shortly before they left for India for their three months, medical elective.

Thus began a life-long love affair with the Indian subcontinent!

Although still based in Wales, they have been able to take time off, at intervals, to visit and work in areas of need in India.

For one year they lived in a little, concrete room in the village compound. One of their remits was to spread hygiene messages to the village people. Prevention of diarrhoea was a vital aim, as it killed a lot of children. The lack of basic amenities was a personal challenge to the two Westerners. For the villagers, life was hard, yet Sally and Carl aimed to leave them with better conditions, to enable them to lead healthier, longer lives.

Also, a long association was formed at the Metropolitan Mission, Vijaywada, Andra Pradesh. An orphanage was founded, funded by individuals and churches in the United Kingdom. When one little boy was asked what the biggest difference was in his life since coming to the orphanage, he replied, 'Having food . . . I'm not always feeling hungry anymore.'

4. THE MEDIC

Liz McFarlane

Adjusting her multiple earrings, Liz hoped she was making a good impression on the attractive, young registrar on her ward. She listened intently to his lovely, soft Scottish accent as he made his morning rounds along with another student. Back in the office, she regaled them with some of her notorious pub tales, which had always stood her in good stead before. Her three colleagues remained unimpressed. To her utter dismay, she later found out that they were those born-again Christians – just her luck!

Liz had reached the stage in her life where she was looking for romance, but not at the expense of her beliefs – or rather, unbelief. She would not describe herself as an atheist, but whatever she was, she certainly wasn't pleased to have this 'religious' lot on her patch at work.

'My childhood was wonderful, in so many ways, as I had (and still have) two incredibly loving, guiding parents, with an emotionally secure and financially comfortable home. Holidays were frequent and fun. Every area of my education was encouraged, which gave me so many advantages in life. So why wasn't I happy?

'Even as a little girl I worried about life and death and resolved every New Year to be good. After a few days, I would be back to my old ways of arguing and lying.'

Her mother faithfully took them to church. Unfortunately, the choir and bellringing seemed to have no more relevance than stories about Jewish fishermen! Also the painting at the top of the aisle, depicting a dead man hanging on a cross was, in her opinion, quite frankly, morbid. What that had to do with her life was a complete mystery. She didn't bother much about it, as she could carry on doing the things in the church without people really knowing her personal thoughts. The time came for her friends to be confirmed, so Liz decided to as well. She thought that she was a Christian because she was a fairly good person who went to church.

Slowly, even her church attendance dwindled and parties took over. Boys were far more interesting! Christmas carols were disturbing, however! She loved to sing them but wondered what was the gift God gave in the line of, 'O little town of Bethlehem,' that says, 'How silently, how silently, the wondrous gift is given, So God imparts to human hearts the blessings of His heaven.' What was all that about? Not just a new bike at Christmas! She was often tearful and angry with God because she couldn't understand these things.

Though denying it to other people with every part of her, at times Liz knew there must be some power that had brought her into being – something that would keep her throughout life, and, of course, not let death be the end of it all. She hoped this power would judge those she perceived as especially bad people, but would generally let her do and say what she liked! Naturally, she would be free to make her own moral judgements! How wrong could she be.

'My A-level results came out but they were not quite good enough grades for me to become a vet: another reason to be angry with fate, or God. Perhaps if I had been more interested in physics than boys then God wouldn't have been the recipient of my frustration!

'I chose to study marine biology, instead, at Aberystwyth University. I soon settled in and life was fun, fun, fun! Parties and friends, sports and occasional studying made life a ball. If it seemed good, I did it. Life was to be lived to the full. Buy now, pay later . . . and of course I was in total control . . . or was I?'

The reality of graduating was a shock: debts and disappearing friends! What now? Liz had safely obtained an honours degree, but didn't abandon the world of academia altogether as she applied to study medicine at Cardiff. Having been accepted, she looked forward to five more years of student fun, with the bonus of a job at the end.

What a shock it was to her system! It was inevitable that here would be loads and loads of hard work, but she was totally unprepared for the terrible loneliness.

Liz began a quest to find God. She looked in the pub and parties: no god. She investigated vegetarianism and various environmental campaigns: no god. She avidly read about all the 'ism's – Buddhism, Taoism, Hinduism . . . New Age, yoga, even tarot cards: definitely no god. And then there were those sickeningly nice Christian people on the same course! She knew she wasn't one of them! Nevertheless, she secretly she envied their convictions and lifestyles.

In the midst of this almost frantic search, which led her to grasp at straws unattached to truth, she came to experience grief for the first time in her life when her grandma died.

Liz was thrown into confusion wondering why her grandma had to go and where had she gone? By now Liz had had enough of parties, boyfriends and messing about. She became acutely unhappy with who she was and what she was.

'I remember getting away from everything by going camping in west Wales. I visited St. David's Cathedral, where, sitting in a pew, I felt like shouting out, "God who are you?" On the way out, I read a plaque about St. David and his sacrificial life. I was so angry with Christians I resolved never to become one.'

A few weeks later, Liz was sent to a hospital ward as part of her course. It was there that the attractive registrar first came on the scene. Bitter disappointment, even resentment on Liz's behalf, was the unfortunate outcome of their meeting, as someone let slip that he was a Christian.

The girl who imparted this terrible news received quite a tirade of abuse from Liz. She went on and on but instead of retaliating, the girl just said, 'Why don't you go to church and try it?'

'Never!' thought Liz.

Back home, she mulled it over.

'Well perhaps I will go once and then I will really know what nonsense goes on. I will then be able to win all the arguments as to why it is a waste of time!'

Her next-door neighbours were churchgoers. She knew that because they often invited her and her friends to come along with them. (Also they had declined lots of offers to her type of parties!) The following Sunday she knocked on their door and said brightly, 'Can I come to church with you?'

'My neighbours later told me that when they closed the door, they were so astounded by the request from the party-mad student who they thought was loud and really happy, that they just stood there in shock! I had no idea where they were going but just trotted along after them. The Heath Evangelical Church in Cardiff was totally amazing. I was struck by the age range, ethnic mix, and number of people there. Something was going on in that building that I'd never experienced before. The singing was so joyful; these people sang as though they meant every word. The man at the front, the Revd Vernon Higham, who was elderly and a bit frail looking, was anything but frail in his message. He simply read the Bible, explained it and meant it!

'One particular verse hit me like a bullet! Probably it's not the one that most people, or preachers, would think of as suitable for a person who was hoping to find God, "Be not drunk with wine, wherein is excess . . ."

'Those words struck home and touched a raw nerve within me. My conscience was so pricked that I was acutely aware of all the wrong in my life. Yet in the same verse God gave me the answer.

'"Be not drunk with wine, wherein is excess; but be filled with the Spirit, speaking to yourselves in psalms and hymns and spiritual songs, singing and making melody in your heart to the Lord." (Eph. 5:18-19).

'I understood quite clearly that if I acknowledged my rebellion against God and asked Him to forgive me, He would fill me with His Spirit. Then I remembered the mysterious words of the carol, which talked about a wondrous gift. So this was the gift it was talking about, the gift of faith to believe. God came into my heart and gave me peace from all the struggling. An enormous weight lifted from me. He had shown me the unhappiness of my life, and told me I was a sinner. No one else could have said these things to me. I was too arrogant to accept it from anyone but a perfect God.'

At the end of the service someone said to Liz, 'Will you come back?'

She replied, 'I never want to leave!'

To her surprise, she spotted Andrew, the registrar, in the congregation. Making his way over to her side he casually remarked, 'I've never seen you here before.' The ever-forthright Liz retorted, 'No, but you'll see me again!'

She left the church not really understanding, in expressible terms, what had happened to her, but she wrote in her diary that night, 'Something has changed today.' The very next day she went to a bookshop to buy a Bible. She just loved reading it. It was enjoyable; it wasn't that she felt forced to read it, she actually wanted to.

'The words were meaningful and interesting, totally life-changing. I prayed to God because I knew Him and loved Him. He had revealed Himself to me.

'My life changed. Lots of things, that previously I had thought 'entertaining', became tedious and unpleasant. My values, absolutes, boundaries, and priorities changed. At last it was OK to be a good person. It wasn't dull or weak, but God-honouring.

'God had a few surprises for me, as well! Not only had He stepped into my life in such a dramatic way, but He was also guiding someone else who was praying about direction for his life. Apparently Andrew, the registrar, had gone to church as usual (the same day of my first visit to the 'Heath'). He was feeling a bit low. With a heavy workload at the hospital as well as exams, there was very little time left for anything or anyone else. He had prayed before the service, 'Lord, if I'm to be a single man that's OK but if not, please show me.' He opened his eyes and noticed me sitting opposite him!

'How strange,' he thought, 'that student's never been here before, but she's a beautiful girl!'

One evening that week Liz had stayed late at the hospital as she was 'on call'. Andrew began to speak to her about the Lord Jesus Christ. Liz found herself whole-heartedly agreeing with everything he said.

'I think he was a bit surprised and sceptical about this sudden change in me. The following Saturday he invited me for a walk and cooked a delicious meal – enough to impress any poor student! He then explained that even though he liked me, we couldn't take the relationship any further as I wasn't a Christian. By then, of course, God had completely changed me deep inside so that I was able to exclaim, "But I am a Christian now!" He disappeared and returned with a handful of books and said, "Read these!" '

Liz was eager to read them and came back for more. They were simple, yet profound, explaining how the Lord Jesus had lived the sinless life she couldn't live, then had taken on Himself her wrongdoing which had separated her from God. He died on the cross taking the punishment she deserved. He had then showed His power over death by rising from the dead to be with His Father in heaven to plead her case. She had been made right with God.

'Andrew and I married fifteen months later! We both continue to have faith to believe in God and have a certain hope of everlasting life in heaven. When I graduated we moved to Scotland. Our family is rapidly expanding; we have two little boys and hope for more children.

'Medicine can be a moral minefield, but God has, thankfully, given us goalposts. If we stick to His Word, most decisions are clear or can be deduced. He knows what is good for us. Without Him, our moods, feelings and emotions change like the weather – making it hard to get it right.'

5. THE FOOTBALLER

Hans Segers

Hans Johannes Cornelius Antonius Segers entered this world in October 1961 in Eindhoven, Holland. He came from a very hard-working family. His dad worked at Philips, the multinational electrical company. Practically everyone in Eindhoven works there! In fact, the 'P' in PSV Eindhoven football club, stands for 'Philips' as they have a controlling interest in the club.

His dad was a very keen footballer in his younger days. He even played for the reserves of Eindhoven, the city's other club. Two broken legs, in his forties, finally ended his footballing ambitions. Tonnie, Hans' mother has always been hard working and is much loved by the family. It was a very male-dominated household, as she had brought into the world three boys, Hans, Frank and Marco. The other two were also good at athletics and football but somehow they lacked the competitiveness of Hans. He hated losing. When he was little, he remembers how he would cry when he let in a goal!

Hans did not like school. He would simply refuse to go! Nowadays, he would be diagnosed as hyperactive and given special help to enable him to learn concentration skills. To put it mildly, he was an underachiever. Every year for him was a struggle.

'I suppose I was a bit of a Jack the Lad at school, throwing my weight around and not worrying too much about passing exams. It wasn't good for my education – but ideal training for my later career in England with Wimbledon's Crazy Gang!'

Always up to something, Hans often found himself on regular visits to the headmaster followed by detentions! He could also have been seen playing 'Sir Galahad'. A girl he liked was being chased and snowballed by another lad. Hans met him in a corridor, picked him up, stuck a coathanger inside his jacket and suspended both jacket and wearer on the wall! Legs and arms dangling, that boy would never have imagined that his attacker would one day be world famous – but for other things! And yes, the girl in the incident, Astrid, did go on to become Mrs Segers!

Hans absolutely loved football. He was always selected for teams of his age. Later, he was picked to play for his county, followed by a trial with PSV Eindhoven, with whom he was to stay for six years. At that time they were doing very well in Europe, so he travelled all over with them. In the last six months he actually made it to the first team.

Every time he goes out to play in the big stadia the 'butterflies' come into his stomach. For the goalkeeper, if he makes a mistake, nine times out of ten it is a goal. However, for his part, the goalie could always blame the outfield players because the ball has to go through ten others before him!

Holland couldn't keep Hans though, as he was transferred at the age of twenty-two, to the home of football, England, and in particular, Nottingham Forest. Believe it or not, he was one of only about five foreign players in

England in those early years – now there seems to be about five hundred!

His new club put him on trial status for the first week, but then the manager, Brian Clough, decided he wanted to sign a contract with him. Brian Clough is a legend and, according to Hans, an 'interesting' man! For the first couple of months, Hans was in the reserves. He will never forget his first away match, however. They were going to play West Ham. Brian Clough, or 'Cloughy' as he was known by some, didn't like travelling. Most clubs set off on Fridays, but not Cloughy.

'We all had to go by coach on the Saturday morning,' Hans remembers, 'down the M1 to West Ham's ground.' Everything was all right until they reached the M25 when they hit road works. The lanes merged. Ahead were miles and miles of traffic cones. Albert, the driver, informed the boss that there was no way they were going to make it to West Ham on time. They looked at the traffic and also realised that there was no way off the motorway.

'Cloughy thought about it for a moment, then stopped the coach. Disappearing through the door, he later returned, having removed about ten cones from a lane. Albert was told to "get in there" (the coned-off lane). At first he declined as he thought he would lose his licence. But Cloughy told him, "In you go!" So we did! Passing miles of traffic, after about ten minutes we saw, in the distance, a dreaded police car with flashing blue light!'

The coach was stopped.

The boss had a chat with the policeman and the next thing they all knew, they had a police escort all the way to West Ham, arriving on time!

Hans enjoyed his four years there, despite being injured during his second season. He tore his cruciate ligament and couldn't get back in the first team.

'I had been on loan for three clubs during a two-year period,' recalls Hans. 'Astrid was finding it very hard to settle. Actually we were thinking of returning to Holland.'

The bright lights of London were beckoning, however, for the young Dutch couple, as a call came for Hans to join Wimbledon as part of the infamous 'Crazy Gang'.

New players always received a special welcome – it could be literally anything!

'Mine was at an away match with Sheffield Wednesday. We travelled on the Friday. The usual timetable was – settle in at the hotel, have a good meal, then back to your room to watch "telly" before getting a good night's "kip".' (Hans had definitely begun to master English slang – *kip* in Dutch, incidentally, means chicken!)

There was to be no sleep for Hans, though.

In all innocence, Hans made his way along the corridors until he came to his room.

Without expecting anything untoward, Hans opened the door, switched on the light and found to his amazement that the room was an absolute mess! On further inspection he saw that there was no television and no bed!

The window was wide open which was very strange.

Sure enough when Hans looked out of the window, there, three floors below, was his bed!

Of course the Crazy Gang recompensed the hotel.

Hans' experience was quite light; other newcomers were not so fortunate.

Marriage Problems

To the average fan, Hans must have appeared to have 'made it'. He was a successful footballer blessed with good looks, a beautiful wife and family, nice home and good car. What more could he want? What people saw on the outside was not reflected in his personal life, which was going rapidly downhill. Astrid and Hans were leading largely separate lives. In the evenings Hans would regularly go out with the lads for a pint so he wasn't spending much time with the family.

'I even cheated my wife after matches. I would say, "it's a long journey back from the match – four or five hours," when it was really only two hours. This gave me a couple of hours spare to have a "good" time with the lads.'

Hans ended up not giving Astrid enough attention, which meant that she too did the same, going her own way.

A 'chance' conversation with her hairdresser got Astrid talking and thinking about Christian things. She had been sharing a little of her marriage problems. At one point in the conversation Astrid asked the lady, 'Are you by any chance a Christian?' The lady was so encouraged that Astrid wanted to talk about Jesus, as so many people, these days, seemed to not want to know. Astrid went along with the lady to her church, where she heard more about Jesus. She wanted to become a real Christian so, asking Christ to forgive her, she received Him as her Saviour.

Everything was so new for her but she had a great desire to read God's Word, the Bible. Hans knew nothing of this, as Astrid was a little embarrassed to tell him, especially as he was part of that 'Crazy Gang'. He did notice that she seemed to be reading a book quite often. He couldn't see the title as the book had been covered with wrapping paper. Strange! Hans eventually found out it was a Bible. Knowing Hans' church background was non-existent (he described 'religious' people as sad!) Astrid wasn't too sure how Hans would react to the news that she had become a Christian.

After four or five weeks their marriage was still not too good.

Finally Astrid put Hans on the spot. She said, 'The only way to make this marriage work is for you to become a Christian.'

Hans looked at her, 'What does that mean? What does Jesus have to do with our marriage? It's just us that has to make the marriage – nobody else.'

And that was that.

Nothing else was to be said.

Two weeks later, Hans was in a real state. He realised he couldn't do 'it' by himself. All his life he had been try- ing to do things his own way.

On this occasion he couldn't handle everything any more.

He was desperate.

Astrid's sister was married to a pastor, across the channel, in Belgium.

'Let's go and see your sister, Petra and Adrie, and let's talk to them about our marriage.'

Astrid began to cry.

'That's what I've been praying for - that you will one day want to know more about faith in Jesus.'

So they took the car, went through the Channel tunnel and travelled on up to Belgium. It was obvious that Hans was serious about wanting help. Once there, they talked with Petra and Adrie for hours and hours. At the end of the evening Hans Segers got down on his knees, bowed his head and his heart before God and asked Jesus Christ to come into his life and help him. It was a simple prayer but he really meant it and God heard and answered.

Hans looks back, 'The relief was overwhelming. The weight of things I had done was gone.'

Over the weeks Hans had observed changes in Astrid's life since she had become a Christian. One of the biggest differences was that she was able to forgive Hans for all the things he had done to her and to his children.

'I thought that was amazing. I know that some people walk around with anger in their lives for years and years. I didn't physically hurt my wife, but I had mentally, and yet she could forgive me! I felt such a peace inside and with myself. I wanted to know more and more. I felt really good.'

Hans had so many questions: 'What happens when we die? Why do bad things happen?' When they returned home Hans joined a group who met to learn more about God, the Bible and being a Christian. He had been so afraid about dying but he discovered that God's gift to those who trust in Him is eternal life, in heaven.

'For God so loved the world that He gave His one and only son that whoever believes In Him shall not perish but have eternal life' (John 3:16).

Dawn Raid

Rudely awakened from sleep at 6:30 a.m. by loud banging, Hans Segers walked down the stairs to open the door and stepped into history – the history of a legal nightmare – in the full glare of TV cameras and the whole media circus. Three men and a woman, from Hampshire Police, arrested Hans Segers for conspiracy to defraud bookmakers. They had a search warrant. They turned the house upside down. Hans was told not to speak to his wife in Dutch. Somehow, the children, Brigette and Nick, remained asleep. Hans' head was spinning – what was happening? One moment he was a successful footballer and the next he was a suspected criminal. What was going on?

When the police banged on the door of the Segers' home in March 1995, Hans and Astrid never dreamt that for the next two and a half years Hans would be caught up in an expensive legal court case, with all the paraphernalia of the media circus. He was accused of attempting to fix a number of premiership games so that a Far Eastern gambling syndicate could win huge sums of money by betting on the results. (The whole procedure is well documented in the book by Hans Segers with Mel Goldberg and Alan Thatcher entitled, *The Final Score*: Robson Books Ltd., Bolsover House, 5-6 Clipstone Street, London, 1P 8LT. ISBN 1-86105-106-9.)

In August 1997 a verdict of 'not guilty' was brought in, to the immense relief to all the family. It had taken two trials, the first having resulted in the jury failing to reach a verdict, which meant a retrial. Although he was free to resume his footballing career, he had to face one further ordeal, a disciplinary hearing by the Football Association. It was claimed that he had breached regulations concerning gambling on matches. Although Hans wasn't aware of these rules he couldn't plead ignorance, so admitted his guilt. Again Hans had to suffer the agony and suspense of waiting for yet another verdict. At last the FA came to a decision. Hans was fined and also given a ban, but both were suspended. He was free to carry on working!

During the court case Hans had suffered a problem with his knee. Wimbledon had signed another very promising goalkeeper, Paul Heald, and Neil Sullivan had come back into the side. Perhaps it was time for Hans to move on? A friend and former player with Wimbledon, Keith Curle, spoke to his manager, Mark McGhee, at Wolves, about the prospects of Hans moving to the club. After hearing about the whole situation, including the trial, Mark allowed Hans to play in a reserves match, which they won 3-0. Hans stayed with Wolves in a non- contractual situation until after the court case.

One of the highlights of his footballing career was when Hans was selected to play for Wolves in the sixth round of the FA cup against Leeds United at Elland Road in front of a full house! Wolves were leading 1-0 when, two minutes before the end, Leeds had a penalty, which Hans saved! It was one of the big upsets of the cup.

For Hans it meant that he was no longer the man in the dock, but rather, Hans Segers – goalkeeper.

Now he was making the headlines for better reasons!

Since becoming a Christian, Hans started to walk the life of faith in Christ, but with faltering steps at first, like a young toddler. The court case years taught Hans many lessons. He found that his friends and family supported him, and God did not desert him. Hans' trust in God grew stronger. Prayer was 'real' and verses in the Bible such as, 'Trust in the Lord with all your heart and lean not on your own understanding; in all your ways acknowledge Him and He will make your paths straight (Prov. 3:4-5), became special to him.

News had got around that 'something had happened' to that goalkeeper from Holland!

Sybil Roscoe, while working for BBC Radio Five Live, interviewed Hans. She asked all the usual questions and then asked, 'How did you come to faith?'

Hans couldn't believe his ears – it was going out live and he was given the opportunity to tell thousands of people how Christ had died for his sins, had forgiven him and was alive in him by God's Holy Spirit!

One memorable phone call which came after the interview, was from ITV, asking Hans if he would be willing to go a meeting, at a stadium in Paris, to share his story of how he came to faith in Christ and to pray a public prayer. The World Cup Final was to be played there one week later and ITV were going to be broadcasting a service from there.

A surprised Hans asked Astrid if she fancied a trip to Paris!

It's amazing who watches the 'religious' programmes on television or rather, who is brave enough to admit to doing so! Through attending that special service in France, Hans was to see another of his private prayers answered, that of where to go next in his footballing career.

Hans had been trying all sorts of avenues since being released by Wolves at the end of the 1997-8 season. Perhaps he should return to Holland or look at second or third divisions? He had telephoned managers and agents galore, but all doors seemed closed for one reason or another.

Two days after the television programme from Paris, the director of football at Tottenham Hotspur phoned to say that he had seen Hans on the morning worship service on TV. It made him think that there could be a position at Spurs for Hans, as cover for the two goalkeepers, plus coaching!

So began a very happy partnership with the London club. When George Graham arrived from Leeds to take over as manager he offered Hans the position as full-time goalkeeping coach.

Hans Segers is involved with 'Christians in Sport'
PO Box 93, Oxford OX2 7YP
Web: www.wat.co.uk/~Christians_sport
Email: stuart@christiansinsport.org.uk
For further information please contact:
hanssegers@yahoo.com

6. THE GAMBLER

John Searle

The sudden, sharp shrill sound woke John Searle from his deep sleep. He felt too weary to switch off the offending alarm clock, so he lay, eyes closed, until his wife nudged him in the ribs.

'Will you do something about that racket?' she said. 'Have some consideration for once – I'm exhausted. It's 2.30 in the morning!'

He felt for the clock and found the button.

Silence.

He lay quite still, wishing he didn't have to go; poker was such a sordid grind.

It had seemed the perfect answer in the old days. It had been an open door to that freedom he had always longed for – no boss, no obligations, plus a carefree, flashy life, following the card game, wherever it could be found.

He saw, in his mind's eye, the room where the 'action' would be. Thick, dirty blankets would be nailed over the sealed windows. Stepping over a greasy carpet you would be engulfed by the dense haze of cigarette smoke, which clung to your clothes. A naked light bulb would be hanging over the green baize of the table. Six pallid gamblers, hypnotised by the drone of the dealer's voice, would be piling up their money, encircled by playing cards.

'The whole picture was exactly like a ghostly scene picked out by a searchlight in a fog. They were animated corpses, trapped in a loveless world. I must go and plunder them without pity, as though in fulfilment of some death wish of theirs,' thought John Searle. They were compulsive gamblers and he was a parasite who fed on their compulsion. He was called a 'professional'.

'Are you awake?' his wife asked.

He didn't answer. He just lay still.

'Are you going, or not?' she wanted to know.

'How much have we got?' Maybe I could put if off for a few days, John thought.

'Two hundred and seventy,' she said, 'and we've got bills for over six hundred, and then there's Angela's birthday . . . '

There was a silence. She could tell he was depressed again. The silver, pure moon shone out of the bare, clear sky, right through the windows. It looked so clean, so far away. John remembered something his father used to quote from Solomon's Proverbs: 'There is a way that seems right to a man, but in the end it leads to death' (Prov. 14:12).

His wife turned away from him.

'Suit yourself,' she said, 'I'm only saying we need the money.'

An hour later, John Searle was thirty miles away, nosing around the back streets of a certain town, where a strong game was running. He had an ostentatious motor car – one of those hand-built Bentleys. He parked it a couple of streets away, because the police were always on the lookout. They had raided the last place and closed it down, but they didn't know about No.49, yet.

After a hoarse conversation through the letterbox, the coffee boy let him in. It was all just as he'd pictured, except that someone lay on a burst sofa with his back to the table.

'Done his money,' explained the coffee boy. 'But he don't wanna go home.'

The players made a space for John. He sat down and closed his eyes, trying to calm himself.

'Are you in this hand?' the dealer asked, 'Or are you saying prayers again?'

'I'm thanking God for sending six dopes to pay my bills,' he answered.

'You shouldn't say that,' a shy Catholic boy murmured. 'That's blasphemy. It's a sin.'

'Shut up!'

John was irritated. 'What do you know about sin?'

Thirty hours later John Searle was still there. He had smoked sixty cigarettes and his head was hurting with the pressure of relentless concentration. He had been in trouble, borrowed five hundred pounds, paid it back, and now he was almost even. Just one good hand and he would be off.

But all at once an inexpressible sense of warmth flooded over John, filling him with a familiar yearning.

'Is that ten to five?' he asked, looking at his watch. No one answered. 'Is it afternoon or morning?' John said. (Because of the blankets at the windows, it was impossible to tell unless you went outside.)

'It's morning, why what's wrong?'

'My mother's awake,' John said. 'You'll have to deal me out. She's praying for me.'

No one laughed.

Someone looked down and almost imperceptibly crossed himself.

The sun was coming up as John Searle drove home. A morning mist was rising eerily from the fields.

'I want to be free,' John said aloud. His heart felt like a dead lump. Tears trickled over the stubble on his face. He seemed to see his mother, with her earnest face looking upward in the way in which he had seen her so many times before, hands clasped, kneeling at her old rocking chair, lips moving – always praying.

His life now was a far cry from his childhood days. He had been brought up in a deeply religious home with loving parents, whose lifestyle could not have been more opposite to that which he had chosen when he eventually left home.

There was just enough space in the room, which was their living/dining/sitting room, for his brother, his two sisters and their father and mother to kneel, in a semi-circle around the fireplace, each evening to pray. They lived in a council house in an industrial city in Yorkshire. It was wartime. Their father was a preacher and often he would be away from home for weeks at a time. They lived ' by faith', which meant that they had no visible means of support, only prayer to God that He would supply their needs.

'We'd pray for everything . . .,' John remembers, '. . . shoes, clothes, food and money for the rent and rates. Our parents were actually missionaries. They were hoping to go back to Central Africa, where they had met in the 1920s after going out to join a missionary work called WEC, which was pioneered by C.T. Studd. (He was an aristocratic gentleman, who played test cricket for England. His name appears on the famous urn, supposedly containing the ashes of English cricket following defeat by the Australians. He was converted to Christianity and gave up a promising sporting career to work as a missionary in China, India and Africa.)

After nine years in Africa, John's mother was physically burnt out. They returned home and were waiting for her to regain her health and strength. She always longed to return to Africa.

'There was a harmonium in our sitting room,' John says, 'and an inlaid, snap-top, walnut, dining table, which our father had bought for 2/6d. There was an old, sprung rocking chair and a sideboard. I remember the rocking chair best of all. It was mother's praying chair. I used to peek at her through my fingers when we were praying. There was no one who was as real to her as God. I would secretly observe her with an unerring instinct for the genuine, which would one day make me such a ruthless poker player. When one of us children was praying, her face was a picture of concentration, of lively interest and love. You could tell that she was actually sharing in our prayers. She would nod and smile or frown to God as if she could see Him.'

One night, during the Second World War, John remembers being woken by an air raid siren.

'I dreaded hearing it. It was like a long drawn-out cry of panic, and when at last it faded away, it sounded like someone dying. I heard the bombers coming from far away, like a warning rumble of thunder in the distance and soon the whole world seemed to be shuddering in fear, as the heavy planes came down low over the city. Why were they flying so slowly? I wondered. Huge explosions began to follow one another until the bedroom window rattled in its frame. I slipped out of bed and crossed the room on tiptoe. I pulled the curtain aside, and there was the city, all ablaze, it seemed. Searchlights swept the sky and anti-aircraft guns sent futile shells streaming out into the blackness. All the time, fresh explosions burst in balls of flames and in the firelight you could see buildings scattering and crumbling into dust. It was just like hell I thought, and I began to scream.

I stood in the pitch dark in the middle of the room, quite sure the world was ending and we'd soon be engulfed in hell.

My mother came in.

She put on the light, and picked me up. I buried my face in her long hair. I remember it as though it was yesterday. (Our father was away preaching somewhere).

'Don't be frightened,' she soothed. 'Don't cry. Our heavenly Father's watching over us, He won't let the bombs harm us.' '

Every day the family learned a Bible verse. Morning and evening they prayed together. Each evening a Bible story was explained to the children. Although they were poor, they were always well fed and clean and well dressed. The house was kept spotlessly tidy: never a speck of dust, no dish or cup was out of place. The father was wonderfully clever with his hands and lovingly made the children birthday and Christmas presents, from salvaged timber. On Sunday afternoons, a Sunday school would be held in their sitting room. The children were expected to knock on doors and invite other children to learn about Jesus. John knew some people in the street didn't like them. One day, he was walking to school, along a deserted lane, with a friend. A man who lived in their street came towards them. He was a tall, gangly man with red hair and big hands.

'Hello, Tommy,' he said to John's friend, 'Why are you pals with that holy Joe?'

Tommy looked confused, even a bit guilty. 'Who's a holy Joe?' he asked.

'He is,' said the man, pointing at John. 'You can't trust holy Joes, Tommy, they're worse'n spies.'

'Are you a holy Joe, John?' Tommy asked, his eyes narrowing with the suspicion of an interrogator.

'Nah, not me,' John said defensively.

'Yeah,' said the man, 'Course he is! Smack 'im one, Tommy, 'fore 'e smacks you one!'

John saw Tommy's fist clench.

He looked belligerent.

John felt a terrific surge of anger.

Suddenly he was sick of being different; sick of this undercurrent which was always there. No one in the street really understood or liked them. He was ashamed of all this reading the Bible and praying – always talking about God.

'You are a holy Joe intya?,' Tommy said menacingly.

Somehow it seemed an appalling thing to be – something that deserved to be crushed and beaten.

'You smack me one, and I'll flatten you, Tommy,' John said through gritted teeth.

'Go on Tommy,' shouted the man. He seemed violently excited.

'Smack 'im one, Tommy! Smack the holy Joe right 'atween the eyes!'

John Searle was afraid and very angry. Tommy bent backwards and before he knew it, John sat astride him, punching and punching.

'I remember his nose bursting and bleeding and the man roaring and swearing. I remember the pain as he caught me by the hair and dragged me off and away from Tommy. He swiped me with a terrific blow on the ear, so that I went staggering sideways into a wall with my head spinning. The man hated me. He cursed me with fearful venom, though I'd never even spoken to him before. I remember the hatred and that I was afraid of it; I was determined to avoid it all costs.'

John's father had (and still has) a faith, which relishes practical challenges. It's active – at its best when on the attack. One day, he came home from a tour of meetings and announced that he was looking for a mansion. There was a desperate need, he felt, for a home for the children of missionaries. It was his deep conviction that God had called him to be used as the means of meeting that need.

His wife wasn't impressed!

She wanted to go back to Africa – back to the place where God had originally called her, while only a schoolgirl. Besides, her faith was already at full stretch. It was all she could do to trust God for their daily needs, which were augmented by the hens' eggs and their homegrown vegetables. If the rent and rates of the little council house were a struggle, how could she be expected to take responsibility for other people's children?

'. . . and exactly how many children . . .?'

'Oh, about thirty,' said Mr Searle, vaguely.

'. . . and where is the money coming from to buy this mansion?'

'From God, of course. He'll provide it!'

One day, John's father came home and triumphantly announced that he'd found the very house they needed. It was stone-built, set in three acres and the King and Queen had been entertained to dinner there. Called 'The Elms,' it was on the outskirts of a seaside town on the East Coast of Scotland and it was on sale for £3,100 (quite a substantial sum in those days!). That evening as they knelt to pray, John was full of excitement. It never occurred to him that his father's vision might not materialise. It was just a question of asking God to send the money; so they did and He sent it – two separate gifts, one of £3,000 and one of £100, earmarked as money for a home for missionaries' children. It seemed absurd to move into such a place with only a few bits of furniture, no money whatsoever, and no means of support except faith in God. But John's parents were to run that home for twenty years, and care for sixty children in that time. He would see daily evidence of God's faithfulness and daily miracles, far too many to record and yet, in secret, his heart was closed to God.

It was painfully obvious to John that he was different from the rest of the family. They knew it too. He was not a Christian, but they all were. Each of them had asked Jesus Christ to 'save them', unlike him. His behaviour was disruptive. He was disobedient. Partly to please the 'Elms' lot and partly to get them off his back, he did the 'right thing' and asked to be 'saved'. If he had expected to hear the voices of angels and that kind of thing, he was disappointed! He felt no different; but there again, he could not honestly say that he was being serious or genuine. He concluded that, really, he was beyond redemption and that he was no good, but he decided that he must pretend and so he walked out looking as peaceful, joyful and satisfied as he could, under the circumstances.

It only worked for a short time, of course. Like everyone else on earth, John was possessed of an unholy spirit by nature, a spirit, which, very soon, made short work of his new image. Because it had all been sham on his part, his behaviour soon deteriorated. Truancy was his chief joy. He began to be possessed by a strange longing for loneliness. It seemed to him that if he was by himself, he was free. There was nothing to compare with that surge of relief he felt when he would steer his bicycle towards the countryside, or the seashore, instead of to school. He'd stand on the pedals, straining for speed as his heart beat faster with the thrill of lawlessness. The consequences didn't matter. Anyway, he could pinch some 'Elms' headed notepaper and forge his excuse. All that mattered was to be out and away. He spent days walking among rock pools, or climbing around the cliffs, or just wandering in the empty countryside.

One Saturday, all the 'Elms' children cycled to a fishing village about three miles away. They were going to play games, and have a picnic on the seashore. Two of the staff came with them to supervise. They started playing rounders, which John thought was boring, so he persuaded a boy to come bird-nesting with him. They climbed a steep path and wandered off along the cliff top. Pretty soon he saw a fulmar or petrel, sitting on her nest on a ledge, just ten feet or so below the cliff top. The tide was on the ebb and more than one hundred feet below the nest, he could see massive humps of wet rock. The first twenty-five feet or so of the cliff sloped slightly outwards, then dropped sheer away, so that you couldn't see the last hundred feet. It was extremely dangerous (and foolish) to attempt to climb in that particular place, where the rock was so soft and crumbly – but the petrel's nest was irresistible. His friend's fearful pleading only added to his bravado. John thought he would show him just how courageous he was. He eased himself over the edge and began the short descent to the nest. The bird gave a sharp cry of complaint, and slipped away, gliding out across the sea. John's friend wouldn't stop talking. John wished he would be quiet. A sudden sense of doom came over John. He knew he was going to fall.

'Come back up,' called his friend, sounding worried and nervous, 'It's too dangerous!'

Stones and crumbling sandstone, which had loosened, bounded down the steep cliff face and vanished beyond the blunt promontory. John couldn't find a solid foothold anymore. His hands were grasping two sods of coarse grass. He just clung there, paralysed with fear.

'Oh, please come back up here,' said his friend.

'Be quiet,' John told him, 'Don't talk to me!'

'Why?' he said, 'Are you all right?'

'I'm going to die!'

John suddenly had a terrible sense of the inevitability of death. Sandy soil trickled into his face from the roots that were holding all his weight. Suddenly they tore loose, launching him backward into space.

'I remember, clearly, the sheer speed and the violence of it as I bounded and flew over the bulge in the cliff. I saw rock and sky and sea all at once, and in my head there seemed to be a deafening cacophony of angry seagulls.

'I cried out with all my heart and soul, 'God save me!' I've often said since that it was the most fervent prayer I ever prayed!

'In a blinding flash, faced with death, if I'd had the time, I'd have promised God anything, if He'd only let me live.'

The cliff was cut away where John fell, because many years before, there had been a narrow landslide. How it happened he doesn't know, but somehow he hit the steep slope below the promontory at exactly the correct angle, so that he broke no bones, but hurtled through a sparse wind-flattened patch of briar and bramble which broke his fall. Rolling over onto the rock of the foreshore, John lay on his back, looking up at the sun. He honestly thought he was dead. It seemed so quiet and hot. And then from far away, he heard the voice of his friend, calling his name. It sounded like a desperate sobbing 'John,' he was crying, 'John, John, John!' As far as John's friend was concerned, all hope had gone. He couldn't see John at all. He raced along the cliff top and ran down the steep path to the picnic place. 'John's been killed', he yelled, 'He's dead, he's fallen from the top to bottom of the cliffs, he's dead!'

The place where John lay was in a bay, encircled by sheer cliffs. He couldn't be reached until the tide was out, but his brother plunged into the sea and swam round to find him.

'I think I am all right,' John said, 'but my head's so hot.'

Together they made it back home; he sneaked unseen into the house and went quickly to bed with the curtains drawn. He wasn't even bruised anywhere. He had no aches or pains, just a vivid memory of fear, and a strange unholy reaction – a sense of resentment that he'd been so thoroughly exposed by desperation.

The children came back from the picnic. Shortly afterwards his mother came into his room. She asked what had happened. He told her as she sat on the bed. She gently stroked his hair and told him something he has never forgotten:

'Your life's been preserved for a purpose,' she said. 'You were spared by a miracle of grace. God has His hand on you John.' She prayed for him, giving thanks. He said 'Amen', but he didn't want God's hand on him. Really he wished He had taken it away – now that he was safe and sound. He just wanted to be free.

As he grew older, John's resistance hardened. He was on a downward spiral. At seventeen years of age he was uncontrollable and totally at loggerheads with all authority. He hardly ever went to school, and when he did, he was insolent and disruptive. One morning he came home at about two o'clock. His father was away in America at the time. John had probably had a bit to drink. The house was in darkness. He went into the kitchen to get something to eat. It was a huge room with a flagstone floor. Between the pantry door and a cupboard, his mother had found space for the old, broken rocking chair they had brought from the little council house. She had knelt at that chair to pray so many times (a picture that was to be etched forever in his memory). As he turned on the kitchen light, his eye caught a movement in the corner. There she was on her knees at the rocking chair, hands clasped, pouring out her heart to God. John was furious. He knew she had a weak heart. The room was chilled and the stone floor hard and cold. She should be in bed. He shook her shoulder. She opened her eyes and looked at him. He glared down on her in a rage. Her face was like an angel; he couldn't bear it. He shouted at her to leave him alone. She said she must pray for him and that he couldn't and wouldn't ever stop her. John wanted to curse her, although he really did love her.

John Searle knew he had made a mess of his schooling; he felt he was a failure, a disgrace. What was to become of him? He was eventually packed off to the RAF. Maybe it would make a man of him. Although he possibly thought that he had escaped the influence of a godly home, when he opened his suitcase on his arrival at RAF Cardington, there on top of his clothes lay a Bible! His mother must have slipped it in.

In the bottom right-hand corner of the flyleaf, there's a date – 14th November 1949. The Bible had been a birthday present when he was twelve years old. John had been hoping, and actually praying for an air rifle. The Bible cost 22/6d. The price is still legible, neatly and discreetly pencilled in the top corner of the page facing the flyleaf. An air rifle would have cost 27/6d – just another five bob! John confesses that he secretly resented the Bible. He also admits that since that day, all those years ago, he has owned and lost all the material things he ever set his foolish heart upon, but somehow, that little Bible never got lost or sold!

'This book of the law shall not depart . . .' was part of the verse his mother wrote in the front, and that's the way it had turned out. Not that he ever really wanted to keep the Bible. For the first thirty-five years, at least, while he lived the footloose life of a professional gambler, his ownership of it was like a penance of dutiful embarrassment. He treated it with grudging reverence, not for what it was, but for what it symbolised.

John had signed on for five years in the RAF and hated it. He had never known such senseless discipline, such suffocating captivity. He longed with all his heart to be free. After only twenty months he was discharged, unfit for service. That was the happiest day he had ever known!

He was nineteen: a misfit, no trade, no educational qualifications and no future.

Every Saturday night, John was off out to buy a packet of fags, have a few drinks and go dancing. In fact, the idea seemed to be that you walked some different girl home every week; but there was, deep inside him, a longing for a stable, truly loving relationship. He grew tired of the restless merry-go-round of different female companions. He wanted to meet someone 'nice', someone 'respectable' and innocent and one Saturday evening he did.

He could tell at once that here was a girl with that guileless, caring charm which expressed itself in genuine sympathy for the oppressed and the deprived. Here was a girl, who, he learned later, had, at the age of ten, cycled seven or eight miles to a farm, to save a litter of cross-bred pups from being drowned. He sensed straight away that she was exactly that kind of girl. He remembers, as though it was last Saturday night, the first time he put his arms around her. They were saying goodnight. She pushed her cheek into his neck and gave a loud sigh, as if they'd been looking for each other for years and they had met at last. John felt like a real man, strong and worthwhile. As he walked home across a park, he looked up at the moon; it was high and bright. The sky seemed like a midnight-blue curtain, stretched right over the world. Beyond the curtain was a glittering kingdom. The flashing stars and the moon were just holes in the curtain, to let the light through from the great, bright world beyond. He knew all that was non-sense, of course, but he felt there was something new and promising ahead.

'I've met the girl I'm going to marry,' he shouted to no one in particular!

John was in love. He was a young fellow with no qualifications, no trade and no prospect of a decent job in a town where his reputation seemed irredeemably tarnished. He was a black sheep, made to look all the blacker because of the impeccable character of his twin brother. He drifted from one temporary job to another; from street photographer to brush salesman, labourer to shop assistant, tunnel man on hydro schemes to semi-skilled engineer, all in the eighteen months between meeting and marrying his sweetheart.

A nagging restlessness, as well as the unwelcome attentions of disgruntled landlords and creditors, drove the newlyweds from one area to another, until they found themselves far from home, living in one room in a dismal house in the city of Glasgow. They had also become the hopelessly irresponsible parents of a baby boy. John found work as an under-manager in an under-wear factory – a drab Victorian building in Maryhill, approached along streets of menacing squalor.

A whole spring and summer escaped his notice. The management staff were like people imprisoned in a nightmare. They would arrive each morning at 7.30 and it was as though they had all left heart and soul else-where, as they plunged into the day's business, which was the churning out of hundreds of dozens of ladies' foundation garments! By 7.31 a.m. the machines were roaring at one another. Everyone had to shout into each

other's ears to pass on vital information concerning production, every couple of hours. People nodded, smiled
and held their thumbs up if everything was on schedule;
they would laugh and slap one another on the back if they
were ahead. If some unforeseen circumstance had robbed
them of their target, everyone would frown, shake their
heads and wring their hands like men bereft! Several hundred women, many of whom were married to drunkards
and who were the sole family breadwinners, would
crouch over their machines with a desperate concentration which still brings a lump to John's throat even now.

'I remember their names – I see them in my mind's
eye – some with bulging hair curlers covered with head
scarves – Sadie, Ina, Betty, Bridie, grinding away in the
thick atmosphere, white with dust, as we, the management, ducked and fussed among the machinery, count-
ing and worrying. We were all caught up in it. No sun-
light for us, no fresh, fluttering wind, no rain or birds'-
nesting time, no hawthorn or blackberries – just this
endless futile mania with production figures. Nothing
else mattered.'

But Sundays were different! John and his wife would
walk around the city. In his arms he would carry his
young son. His wife's shoes had holes in them. She had
no coat, because they had pawned it, along with her
engagement ring, to buy food for the baby. John just
couldn't stay in, though, so he and Stella would roll
some cigarettes, as thin as matchsticks and go off on
their journey into dreamland. She'd look at expensive
furniture stores. But for John it was cars. He loved them!
In fact he worshipped them.

John recalls a childhood incident that sparked off that
initial interest:

'During the war, on the way to church one Sunday,
we'd passed a little two-seater car, parked at the road-

side. I was about five or six years old. I remember that it was black with a red interior, and the top was folded down, out of sight. I stopped, fascinated by the array of instruments and the open cockpit.

'"That's an MG," my father told me. "It can do 80 miles per hour."

'"What does that mean?" I asked.

'"That's very fast," he said. "If you got in it now and drove full speed until we came out of church, you'd be more than 80 miles away. Come on," my father said, pulling me away, "you can buy one when you grow up!"

'I didn't want to leave the MG. I just wanted to stand there and look at it and think about it. I loved the feeling it gave me.'

So there they were, hardly able to exist in a grimy, prosperous city, spending their Sundays window shopping like two children. Rolls Royce and Bentley, Jaguar, Jensen – they visited the showrooms one by one, always saving the best till last. John was working himself up to visit Callanders; they sold Aston Martins. John would stand at their showrooms with his baby son under his arm, his face so close that the window would steam over. Ten minutes would pass, even twenty sometimes. The seeping drizzle would chill them all to the bone, but John never noticed the rain, or his wife patiently waiting, knowing in her heart how the longing for fast cars utterly possessed him.

'I'm getting ever so wet,' she said one day. 'Can we go home now? My shoes are letting in the rain.'

John turned and looked at her. He could tell she understood.

'I'll get an evening job,' she said. 'Save every penny, you'll see. I'll wash dishes, or scrub floors. Only please, don't be so unhappy.'

John didn't deserve her. He knew that well enough. He felt ashamed. The whole compulsion of his life was self-interest.

'I was a monumental egotist,' says John, ' but little did I know that one day I really would own my Aston Martin. Meanwhile I would open my mother's letters, hoping for a pound or two, and then, can you believe it, throw them in the bin, unread.'

One day John actually went to church. He was having one of the battles, which erupted now and then, out of the state of constant war that always seemed to be rumbling away somewhere in his soul. When he was sure his wife wasn't looking, he would sometimes read his Bible. He loved the language, but couldn't really understand why he read it! It was as if he was doing something shameful – even wrong. He would wait until his wife was in the bath or out shopping and then sneak away to read it. At the back of his mind was the thought of what would happen when his mother died and her prayers were silenced.

'I was afraid, but self-preservation was my main concern, so we went to church, just once. I really believe that I did want to somehow be convinced. If only God would stop me short in my tracks – give me no option – take my heart by storm – even strike me down, just so that I could know His personal concern for me.'

But nothing happened.

John and Stella left Glasgow in a panic. They couldn't even wait until dark; their creditors were closing in. John had bought a vast, ancient eight-seater American Packard car, even though he had no driving licence. Wearily, they loaded the old limousine with their earthly goods, in broad daylight. They had sold all their furniture, though they had made no payments on it, in order to buy the car and put a deposit on a caravan.

The car took them just less than one hundred miles before a spectacular mechanical explosion consigned it to the junkyard. They ended up in a lay-by, at the roadside, in the Awe Valley, living like perennial wayfarers in their caravan. John managed to get work as a tunnelman once more.

There they were, with no fixed abode, no running water and no electricity. John worked like a dog seven days a week, twelve hours a day and every evening after dinner he would be out fishing for trout, until dark. His poor wife would sit in the caravan under the towering mass of Ben Cruachan, which seemed to threaten her, and frown upon her. Every day she washed the baby's nappies at the lochside, laughing and complaining, as the wind, which seemed to roar endlessly through the funnel of the Awe Valley, blew her soapsuds away.

As darkness fell the caravan would shudder in the gusts, and the crockery would rattle in the cupboards. Sudden rainstorms would rush down the valley and strike the aluminium caravan with a heavy slap, like the rebuke of a giant hand. John would come home, with a bag full of trout, oblivious to the weather, to find his trembling wife curled around her son, as though to protect him from evil.

'I'm afraid, John,' she said 'and I am lonely.'

But he didn't care, really. In fact he laughed at her. He told her that his mother had trekked alone through the Ituri forest, in darkest Africa, when she was only a young woman.

One evening, he arrived from work late to find the caravan empty.

There was a note on the table.

'I didn't want to read it. The writing was out of focus. I kept staring at the paper.

'She was pregnant again.

'She'd had enough.

'She still loved me with all her heart, the note said, but she couldn't 'bare it' any more.'

John started laughing.

'That's not how you spell "bear it".' He said aloud.

Stella had gone hitchhiking home to her mother, right across Scotland, with their baby.

The wall light guttered and changed from white to blue. The place grew dim, then dark. The wind moaned in the ventilator.

'Please God – help me,' John called out, then sat down and descended into self-pity.

'I want to be free.'

But no one seemed to be interested.

'There's nothing which more effectively deceives a man, in my experience, than self-pity. It blinds him utterly to the true state of his own heart. It's a stepping stone to self-justification, which is the tap root of all kinds of evil,' reflects John in retrospect over this sorry period of his life.

His wife had left him. She'd let him down, he felt. How could she have been so selfish! 'There I was, in that cramped, tinpot caravan, without light or fuel, stuck in a narrow lay-by in the gathering gloom of the Awe Valley. Meanwhile, she was safe and comfy at home with her mother on the opposite coast of the country, as far away from me as she could get.'

'What I fool I am!' he thought. 'There I was, all along, thinking she loved me! Well, I'm no saint, but I'd never have deserted her! Never!'

He felt faithful, noble and aggrieved. Not a single thought, mind you, of those endless evenings when he had left her alone while he fished for trout until after dark! John walked to the village and bought a bottle of whisky. He opened it and took a deep swig. Horrible! He didn't drink much. He hated it, but what does a man do when his wife's forsaken him! Too windy and too late to go fishing – besides, he would not enjoy it, knowing Stella wouldn't be there when he returned. The caravan shook in the teeth of a violent gust – a storm was coming. He could hear the roar of heavy rain, sweeping down the loch. It was one of those times when you got the feeling that you're the only person on earth.

A huge ball of thunder seemed to crash into Ben Cruachan and burst right above him, as though the little caravan was at the epicentre of a great explosion. The echoes went rolling away through the valley.

'Is that you out there?' he said, 'Are you there, God?'

'If only I knew for certain then I could pray properly, like mother.

'But it's no use.

'God has no time for the likes of me. I am doomed, just like Judas.'

John Searle was soon reconciled to his wife and child. Not long after, their son was born. John pretended to be pleased, but really, John was in a bad way. Looking back, he can remember awful things – things that make him shudder now. Certainly some irrepressible evil influence seemed to have possessed him. He was a restless, totally self-centred bully, blatantly unfaithful and utterly callous. There wasn't a single redeeming feature in his nature.

One day, Christians were preaching in the street where John had moved to live with his wife and family. He had acquired a little pre-war two-seater MG, exactly like the car he had coveted and fallen in love with when he was a child. It had a very sporty exhaust noise, and so when the meeting got going, John started the MG and revved the engine, drowning out the hymn singing and the message. Afterwards, one the students came to speak to John. He didn't seem angry or put out by the rudeness; in fact he was calm and respectful. He had an air of kindness and confidence about him, which made John ashamed of his own senseless hostility. John actually invited him to come into the house, and there they sat talking for hours, until well after midnight. John could see quite clearly that he had a spirit of power, love and a sound mind, which made John envy him.

When he had gone, John was filled with a long-forgotten yearning that he thought had gone forever – the precious ministry of the Holy Spirit who convicts men of sin – the gracious initiative of a truly loving God. He felt unclean. All the meanness of his nature was revealed to him – the sheer madness and cruelty of sin, which enslaved him.

John looked at his wife. She hadn't said a word all evening, but just sat looking at him, beseechingly. She hadn't even understood the conversation – she just longed for something better. He knew she trusted him, looking to him for guidance in everything. She was innocent and unsophisticated, but he had betrayed her. He had even tried to urge her into extra-marital relationships, in order to excuse his own flagrant infidelity. She was confused and desperately unhappy and he knew that he was destroying her.

It reminded him of a verse from the Bible, 'The thief comes only to steal and kill and destroy' (John 10:10).

As children, they had been taught to learn verses from the Bible daily, which from time to time would come back to him. (Later on when he was gambling, he did very well because he had a good memory.) But it's one thing to recite something and quite another to believe and receive it. John just couldn't seem to believe there was mercy in the heart of God for the likes of him. He found his Bible and looked up Isaiah 53. As he read the familiar phrases aloud, the opening words of verse 9 seemed to stand out in bold, 'He made his grave with the wicked'.

'I said it again. I kept repeating it. My wife was staring at me, wondering what was going on. I shouted it out – "He made his grave with the wicked".

'"That's me," I said. "This whole chapter's really about people like me. I'm going to kneel down and pray for God's forgiveness, and ask for His power to live a new life."'

She didn't really understand what he was talking about, but he did it, and at that moment, he meant it. He wanted it all to be true for her and for him. But John felt nervous and apprehensive, right from the start. He knew he was expecting some tremendous thing, and somehow he doubted if it was really going to happen.'

He lit a cigarette and put the kettle on. Before they had finished their coffee he had smoked two more.

'You are nervous,' Stella said to him. She looked nonplussed and a bit worried.

'So would you be if you realised what I've done,' he told her. 'I'll have to go round and tell my parents in the morning.'

But it was already morning. Dawn was breaking. One more cigarette and then he would go to bed.

His parents were overjoyed. He went along with it all, deeply touched by the love, which was implicit in their thanksgiving to God. He joined in singing songs, swept along on the almost irresistible tide of his parents' relief. Maybe he should even become a preacher?

One day he met a girl he had flirted with, now and then. About six weeks had passed since that momentous night when he had tried to surrender his life to Christ. She told him she had heard that he had gone off his rocker.

'Yes,' he said, 'Maybe I have. I'm going to be a preacher.'

'What a waste,' she said 'whoever would fancy a preacher?'

Suddenly he began to feel like that man who set off to sail around the world, a few years ago. He enjoyed a tumultuous send-off, but never actually ventured more than a few miles from the coast of England. He just tacked around, out of sight of land, sending fake radio messages. He gave as his position exotic, far-flung places, but there he was all along, sailing up and down the English Channel! At the last, afraid to set out on his epic voyage proper, and ashamed to face the ridicule of friends (and no doubt the wrath of sponsors), he abandoned ship. He threw himself overboard and left his empty boat to tell the tragic tale. When John heard the story on TV News, his heart went out to him in sympathy, feeling that he had something in common with him. As for John, he couldn't even stop smoking! Surely that was just about the first thing a Christian ought to do?

'I seemed to soar to heights of zeal and ambition for God's kingdom so quickly. Where had it all gone? Like a bright firework rocket which has burst in a shower of starry sparks, I had burned up what fuel I had. The enthusiastic send-off seemed to have lost its power. (I did not understand then that it is only by the resurrection power of God in Christ that a person can live as God intends.)'

The magnetic lure of his world drew him downward into the darkness again. He simply didn't want the old life to die. His heart was set on earthly things. John felt that he was a 'black sheep'. Perhaps he had been a fool to think things could have been any different.

As time elapsed, his wife despaired of him. She couldn't bear to be in his company.

Then, one day she disappeared.

John took the children to his mother. He ranted and raved, calling his wife all sorts of vicious names, explaining all her faults and failings to his mother. She listened; she didn't say a word. For ten minutes he indulged himself, justified and pitied himself, cadging sympathy. At last, exhausted, he sat down.

'It's all your fault,' his mother said calmly. 'It's not Stella's fault – it's yours. You've driven her away. You're controlled by the devil and that's the top and bottom of it!'

John returned home, thinking what a cruel body blow his total backsliding must have been to his parents. Perhaps they'd give in now; maybe he would be left in peace. But his mother's heart never fell silent; her prayers just changed in tone, that's all. His mother must have been shaken, even bewildered by it all. But she dug deep. She refused to surrender. Quietly, but with great determination, she prayed on, without ceasing, for twenty-five more years for that wayward prodigal son of hers.

Never underestimate the power of God and a praying mother!

Stella and John decided that their marriage was in a mess. They weren't getting anywhere. Months and years were slipping away. The little history of their lives was like a minefield of bad debts and broken credit agreements. Nothing mattered to John except fast cars and that totally self-indulgent, raw 'blues' music, which seemed to have its roots in the restless, lost soul of deprived humanity. In the first five or six years of their married life, they had moved at least twelve times. By the time their third child had arrived, things hadn't seemed to improve much. The only cars that seemed worth driving, in John's eyes, were those sports Jaguars of the fifties. All essentials would be stuffed into the cockpit and the tiny luggage boot: pots, pans, dishes, sheets and bedding and of course his precious collection of blues records. They would pack the family in, some-how, and, with the hood down, leave town with a shriek of tyres, a litter of bad debt and furious creditors behind them.

The main thing for them, or rather for John, was to be on the move, flat out, in fact. John's philosophy was that if you weren't doing 130 miles an hour, you weren't going anywhere!

But self-delusion is no permanent substitute for the truth.

Life was hell.

No peace, living on tenterhooks, a victim of tempta-tions which seemed irresistible. There had to be changes, they said. Their latest Jaguar had seized up as they were heading home from a fruitless attempt to settle in England. The family just left the car on the roadside and hitchhiked home to 'The Elms'.

For the umpteenth time, they were penniless and des-perate. John had had lots of jobs and many a golden opportunity, but he wasted them all. They had nothing. All their earthly goods and personal belongings had been left behind. John and Stella had been parted and reconciled several times. John truly loved his wife, but there was a terrible power, which would seize him – a ruthless, surging turmoil, which gave him no peace. Satan had plenty of tricks up his sleeve. He had, in John, an eager ally, whose will was his, and he was to find a way of satisfying John's worldly ambitions.

They decided to leave Scotland and make a new start. His dear parents agreed to care for their three children, while they established themselves in England. John had heard of a town where there was plenty of work. A man, whom they knew, had recently moved there. He was living in a caravan behind a village pub. There was room for them as well, he said. John, meanwhile had been working as a car salesman, doing crooked deals for a rather dangerous, moody character who had a thriving business. The job involved blatant, hair-raising deceit. Strictly speaking, it was legal, but he made a lot of enemies.

One dismal, midwinter evening, Stella and John caught the night train to Peterborough. 'The only luggage we had was a carrier bag with those wretched, haunting gramophone records packed in it – but I realise now that we must have taken my old Bible as well, because it's still with me. '

They held hands and looked out of the window, even though there was nothing to see except billows of freezing fog obscuring the street lamps. There had been no sunset that day – just a darkening of the atmosphere. Christmas was over, and they had said goodbye to the children. It was late December 1965.

'I'm glad I'm leaving this dump,' Stella said, 'I'm never coming back.' She sounded angry and defiant, but there were also tears in her eyes.

They counted their money again. They had hardly any. Never mind, it would all be different when they got settled in England, so they thought.

'Scotland's too small for you, John,' Stella said, laughing.

They were hoping that they would both get jobs, rent a nice house and in no time at all they would be a proper family like other people. Their eldest son was only six years old and he was already on his fourth school. They both agreed that it wasn't right. At least now the children would be well looked after.

'It will do them good to live at "The Elms" for a while. Oh, we are doing exactly the right thing,' Stella said. But she was clinging to John's arm ever so tightly. 'If we just love each another, we'll be all right.'

Something deep inside John seemed to assure him that they were truly entering a new phase. He felt optimistic and determined. Things were going to improve. It was a new day, they could tell that. The atmosphere was different. The sun shone as the local train took them to the destination that would change their way of life.

The village where his friend lived was seven miles away. They stood outside the station blowing into their hands and stamping their feet to warm them. They were hungry. A taxi driver sat in this car, watching them. He made a gesture, offering his services. John went over to him and told him where they wanted to go.

'Trouble is, this is all we have in the whole world,' John admitted, showing him their meagre, few coins, 'Can you take us as far as our money lasts? We'll walk the rest.'

'Get in,' the driver said. He switched off the meter and took them all he way. They tried to give him their money, but he refused it. 'Good luck to you,' he said and drove away. 'So this is England!' thought John, 'This is more like it! Didn't I say everything was going to be all right!'

Unfortunately, when they found their friend, he wasn't pleased to see them. They were trouble, or at least, John was. Reluctantly, he took them to meet the landlord, who showed them the only caravan he had for rent. It had no electricity, no means of heating and the inside walls were rippling with damp. There was mould everywhere. The mattress was sodden and there was no bedding, cooking utensils or crockery.

'Three quid a week,' he said. 'A month in advance.'

They agreed and handed over the only money they had. They were both hungry. Shortly, the landlord came back with two bread rolls with a poached egg in each.

The eggs were cold. There was no butter on the rolls, but John and Stella were starving. They tried to light a fire, but dense smoke belched out of the little stove as though it had been just waiting there for someone to strike a match. In desperation, they struggled with the windows that wouldn't open. They went outside, and watched the smoke pouring out of the door.

'Let's go for a walk,' John said 'and wait for the smoke to clear.' Their 'friend' didn't offer them even a cup of tea. He had a proper stove, and a gas heater. He didn't want to know them. But as they stood on an ancient, narrow bridge, looking down at the river, John was glad. He put his arm around Stella.

'We don't need anyone,' he said. 'We'll make it on our own.'

Slowly, they made their way back to the caravan. It smelled horrible. The landlord came and told them off for starting a fire. He gave them two weeks to pay him £18.

'That will put you a month in advance,' he said.

When he had gone, Stella said one of the wonderfully irrelevant things, which seem to come into her head at times.

'Never mind, it will be the New Year in a couple of days.'

John began to laugh. He laughed until he ached.

'What's so funny?' she asked. 'I don't see anything funny. Honestly John, I don't understand you sometimes.'

John wanted to hug her, but she wouldn't let him. That night, as they huddled together, a bitter frost came down. John wrapped her in his overcoat and watched as she fell asleep. Their children were almost five hundred miles away, but at least they were warm and well fed. 'Why am I such a disastrous failure?' John wondered. 'I am supposed to be the provider, the head of the family. Things will surely be different in the future.'

John awoke just before dawn.

The clothes he had slept in were frozen to the wall of the caravan, but somehow he didn't mind the cold.

Stella found a job packing scrubbed potatoes into bags. The vegetable warehouse was just a stone's throw from the caravan, but there was no work for John. He gained the impression that his old friend had soured the management's mind against him. There was nothing else for it – he would have to look elsewhere.

John walked to the nearest town and found the dole office. The clerk seemed to hate him. Reluctantly he gave him a form to fill in. John had told him that he was desperate and was handed some coins.

'If you want to work,' he said, handing John a card with a name on it, 'there's a job at this firm.'

'Twelve-hour shifts: 6 a.m.–6 p.m.,' he said, as if the prospect of such drudgery would make him disappear.

He looked at John's address.

'I hope you know there's no transport – no buses or anything,' he said helpfully.

'Are you going for an interview or not?'

'It's a start,' John said optimistically.

'How are you going to get there for six in the morning?'

'I'll walk.'

'It's hard work, that place – they're always on to me for people.' That was his final encouragement.

'Thanks for the warning,' John called over his shoulder, as the clerk turned away with an irritated tut and a loud sigh before leafing through cards in a metal cabinet.

John got the job. It was on one of those desolate industrial estates. It took two hours to walk home. The roads
were dry, but a north wind was driving heavy snow
clouds from the Arctic. He had bought chocolate with
some of the emergency payment he had received from
the dole office. The chocolate was the only food they had
for supper. By late evening, three to four inches of snow
had fallen. They slept in their clothes. John spent a fitful
night worrying that he might oversleep in the morning
and be late for work. How long would the journey take
in the snow? He worked out that if he had to clock in at
6 a.m., then he had better leave by at least 3.30 a.m.
Wrapping his overcoat around Stella, he slipped off the
bed. It was pitch dark but she reached out and touched
his hand.

'What are you doing?' she demanded. 'Where do you
think you're going?'

'Ssh! – go back to sleep – I'm off to work.'

'You can't go in this, there's no need, besides you'll
freeze to death. I don't want this coat round me, I'm too
hot. Look at that silly thin suit you're wearing and that
horrid nylon shirt and what about your shoes? What use
are they in this weather? Wait till next week. I'll have
some wages then. We can buy some food. You're half
starved. Stop upsetting me. Just leave out all this heroic
stuff!'

'See you tonight,' John whispered, 'don't worry, I've
got some chocolate left from yesterday, there's some for
you as well.'

He felt for the table in the dark and left a thin bar of
mint-filled chocolate for her breakfast. He had to literally kick at the door as he went out, to break the seal of
ice, which held it fast.

John was sick of the trap of poverty. Since earliest
childhood, he had dreamed of freedom. He would

rather walk until he dropped than lie shivering in that caravan. 'Anyway, the cold wasn't too bad, once you got going,' he told himself.

His mind went back to those long-distance men he'd known and worked amongst, who roamed the Scottish Highlands, drifting restlessly from work camp to work camp, when the hydro-electric schemes were under construction. Most of them were Southern Irish men, who fought and drank and worked like folk heroes: free spirits – and he was one of them.

It was all a passing romance, of course, but it would have to do for the moment.

Within two days, John was exhausted. The heavy work was physically demanding. Inside the factory, the atmosphere was thick with dust and heat. On the second night, the walk home was like a never-ending nightmare. A pitiless east wind blew flurries of powdered snow, hissing down out of the dark, which stung his face and ears. John beat his body with his arms. Even though he wrapped his jacket around himself as tightly as could, and turned up his collar, it was of little use. The cold, piercing like thin, icy daggers, found its way in. He was defenceless against it. His old friend, living with the comforts of a gas heater and an oven and electricity, seemed to enjoy John's wretched situation. He had turned against John, who then felt like the prodigal son in the Bible, who 'began to be in need . . . and no one gave him anything'.

John was numb with cold, and still had three miles to go. He was determined to get the money, even if it killed him! He would show them.

When he reached the caravan, he was done in. It was 9.30 p.m. He had been on the road for more than three hours. In six more hours he would be out on the road again, walking back to work. He suddenly felt dizzy. A candle burned in the window, and the condensation trickled and glistened. As he opened the door, Stella jumped up. She had put up the folding table, and there, right in the middle of it, was a pan, almost filled to the brim, with hot, steaming potatoes.

'Where have you been?' she said, throwing her arms around him, 'I was so worried. O, you poor, naughty man, you're freezing. Sit down here. Put this on!' She took off his overcoat, which she had been wearing, and wrapped it around him.

'You're not to do this,' she said. 'I'm not having it. It's not fair on me! You'll kill yourself.'

'Don't be silly,' he told her, 'by the way, where did you get those "tatties"?'

'Nicked them from work,' she said proudly, '. . . and I got the pan "on tick" from the village store – told the man a sob story, but it's true, isn't it? He's the very nicest man! – "Course you can have credit, my dear. My pleasure, you poor children!" That's what he said. They let me peel and boil them in the pub kitchen.'

As they ate the potatoes with their fingers, John began to feel strong and warm.

'Stella,' he said, 'I'm going to make lots of money, because when you've got money, you're free. You can do just what you want. People say money isn't everything, but I know it is. Just let someone come and live my miserable life, and then tell me that money doesn't matter.'

Later, as they lay side by side in the dark, Stella sat up suddenly and looked out of the window. 'It's thick out there,' she said. She lay quietly for a while, and then she spoke her thoughts out loud, 'I wonder if it's snowing in Scotland.' After a minute or two passed, he sensed a deep tension in the silence. She began shaking without making a sound, but he knew that she was crying. As he

put an arm round her, she suddenly cried out with a
loud wail of grief, which shocked and scared him.

'Oh John! My babies! Why have we left our babies?'

John couldn't answer, or even speak at all. She turned
towards him. 'Tell me it's going to be all right, John – tell
me again! We'll have some money and live in a proper
house like a family, won't we! That's right isn't it? Tell
me again!'

'Ssh, we will have a fine house,' John soothed. 'I know
we've lost our things, our furniture and stuff, but we're
starting again. We'll have all new things – better things.
Not only will we have a bedroom for us, but the boys
will have a separate one too and little baby Angela will
have a brand new cot. We will have a proper kitchen
where we can eat breakfast and a garden full of flowers,
with a wooden shed in it where we keep the boys' bikes
and our "wellies", and all the garden tools . . . and we'll
have a posh car – a real fast one that's bought and paid
for this time . . . and we'll go on family holidays to the
seaside and stay in a hotel and we'll look right down our
noses at all the poor folk on caravan sites . . .'

Stella had fallen asleep; she must have been exhausted. As she worked a ten-hour day, she was under terrible stress. But John was wide awake, not even bothering
to try to sleep. A familiar restless energy was in him. If
God really knew his heart, he thought, everything
would be all right, because after all, surely he was only
a poor, silly boy who couldn't help it. Stella caught her
breath suddenly, and then let it out in a long shuddering
sigh, exactly like a little child who had cried herself to
sleep.

As for John, he wished it was 3.30 a.m. He wanted to
be away, out on the road, walking back to work.

'It's the only answer,' he said to himself, 'Get money
and if God's got any compassion or decency in Him,

He'll help me, and then I'll believe in Him and everybody will be happy.'

His first wage was about £14. With money in his
pocket, he found lodgings in a big, dilapidated old
home; about a dozen men lived there. They were mostly
labourers on the roads, weather-beaten men without
roots, who didn't ever say much. The landlord
explained that for breakfast there were cornflakes, two
slices of bread and margarine with marmalade. Six
evenings a week, a cooked meal would be served in a
room adjoining a café, which was owned by the propri-
etors of the hostel. After a fortnight of starving in sub-
zero temperatures, the prospect of a dry room with its
own fireplace and a proper meal each day, except
Sundays, was just about the most enticing thing in the
world. John gladly handed over £7 10 shillings for the
first week's board.

'That's for the two of you,' the landlord said, looking
at him suspiciously. John must have appeared wild and
rough, as he hadn't shaved since leaving Scotland. The
landlord counted the notes in his hand several times.

'Any violence, any breakages or drunkenness or "nick-
ing" from the pantry – any trouble at all, and you're out!'
he said. 'We've never had a woman tenant here before,
but the same goes for your wife, or whoever she is!'

John bought a packet of twenty cigarettes and set off
with the good news. It was to be the very last time that
he would trudge along that road in the freezing dark.

'Wonderful! Steaming "tatties" again!' he exclaimed,
as he hugged his wife.

'But oh, there's corned beef too and some nice fresh
milk to build up your strength. I've been paid, see,' she
added, proudly.

The place was so cold that, in the candlelight, they
could see their breath, like small clouds of freezing fog.

Stella didn't seem to mind. As they sat down opposite one another, John couldn't help thinking that they might just as well have been dining in some faraway café in Venice. He would always love her, he told himself, and never betray her again. Just wait until she heard his news about the lodging house in town!

'Listen,' she said, 'I've got something to tell you. I had great fun today at lunchtime. I told a woman's fortune. All the girls were fascinated. I didn't actually know I could do it, but it's dead easy. You just let yourself go and it all comes out. I told this woman lots of things about herself and her family. She was thunderstruck. Everyone was talking about it. I felt really important. Lots of girls wanted a turn!'

Stella spoke with excitement as she eagerly told him the details. But John didn't want to hear what she was saying. He was uneasy. He felt a sense of foreboding, but as he watched her, he could see that her face looked bright and natural. There was nothing sinister or evil about her – quite the reverse.

John told himself that it was probably harmless, just a lot of superstitious hocus-pocus. Yet warning bells kept ringing in his head, but, surely that was only because of all that religious stuff he had had drummed into him as a child.

He made Stella promise him that she would never mention anything like this to his parents.

'Why not?' she wanted to know.

'They wouldn't understand, that's all.'

'Oh, but it's fun! It doesn't harm anyone! What's wrong with it?'

'I didn't say you had done wrong. In fact it's all a lot of nonsense. Just don't ever mention it to my parents. I'm telling you they'd be upset.'

Stella looked hurt, like a child who didn't understand

why she had been told off. She had enjoyed being
treated like a 'somebody' – but she had taken the first
steps along a road which would lead to terror and the
blackest darkness. She had eagerly surrendered, albeit
in ignorance, to a heady power which had given her
instant status, a kind of authority and popularity. With
hindsight, John later felt that he should have known
better. He ought to have warned her, indeed pleaded
with her and explained somehow that she was in peril.
Perhaps she might have listened; but he couldn't admit
to the 'Truth' he denied. Ten years would pass, years
when there would be almost daily occult 'consulta-
tions'. He vividly remembers arriving home in the small
hours from a poker game, shocked to find Stella sitting
up, staring at an open book held tightly in her hands.
She wasn't reading it – just holding on to it, as if the dis-
traction would protect her mind from some dreadful
thing which was lurking nearby, waiting for her first
unguarded moment so that it could pounce and possess
her. Her face looked blank and numb, as she clung to
her book, afraid to go to bed, afraid even to explain
why.

But back there in that icy caravan, shivering over a
dinner of boiled potatoes and corned beef, John put all
the childhood warnings out of his mind.

'It was obvious what God was up to,' he thought. 'He
was jealous. The Bible admitted as much. He simply
wanted people to be utterly dependent on Him for
everything. That was the whole confidence trick of
Christianity. You couldn't express yourself or investigate
any other system of spiritual fulfilment without the God
of the Bible coming down on you like a ton of bricks. No!
It wasn't fair to bog her down with the hangovers of my
childhood! Let her enjoy herself! Besides, why spoil the
news of new accommodation?'

'We've leaving here tomorrow,' John said. She perked up in a flash. She was instantly alert. 'Where are we going?'

'Oh, I've found the very place,' he said proudly. 'We've to get our food, and it's only £3 15 shillings a week. I've already paid up front. I've found jobs for both of us in a factory nearby and we can save like mad until we've got enough to send for the children.' He watched her absorbing the news, but suddenly a cloud seemed to pass over her face.

'But we owe for the rent here, for this caravan,' she said in a loud whisper as though the landlord might hear. 'He asked for his money when I was in the kitchen peeling tatties. He's expecting it tomorrow.'

'What do you think?' he asked.

She thought for a few seconds 'Skinout?' she asked mischievously. 'You've got it! What's the point of travelling light if you can't have a good quick skinout!'

They began to laugh. They laughed until the tears ran.

'Serves him right,' Stella said with injured dignity, when she'd calmed down. 'Asking hard-earned money for a smelly dump like this! Let's blow the candle out in case he sees the light and comes to call. Hey! Just a minute'. How are we going to get away from here?'

'There's a bus at ten in the morning. It only runs twice a week. We'll sneak off on foot – pretend we're going for a stroll, and flag it down.'

'Just one thing,' she said with self-righteous solemnity, as we lay side by side in the dark, 'I'm going to pay that dear kind man who let us have the pan on tick.' She paused, 'but we'll wait until we're better off.'

They never paid him.

The following evening they stood looking around at their new home. It was a large room, with five single beds and no other furniture. A single, naked bulb hung from the ceiling. There was some brown linoleum on the floor with patches worn away. The plaster had long jagged cracks in it and the lock had been torn away from the door, so that it wouldn't shut unless you wedged it with folded newspaper or something. There were two large windows with threadbare, unmatched curtains. The bathroom was next door. It boasted a mighty over-head Victorian cistern made from ornate cast iron, which thumped like an anti-tank gun when you pulled the chain. You could hear the other residents banging about, getting ready to go out drinking. It was Saturday night.

'Is it safe here?' Stella asked John.

'I can look after you,' he said.

'Why are there so many beds?' Do you think this is someone else's room as well?'

'No, of course not,' he assured her. 'Look, just sit tight. I'm going to find some wood for the fire.'

John managed to find some old seed boxes and a wormy stool in a shed outside. There they sat, two beds pulled together, watching the fire as it roared up the chimney.

'This is heaven,' she said. 'Better than a five-star hotel. You were ever so clever to find this place.'

'The blankets are a bit grubby,' he said doubtfully, 'but compared to that caravan . . .'

'Sh! It's heaven,' she interrupted, 'except that I don't believe there is such a place, do you?'

'There must be,' he told her, 'otherwise where'll my mother go when she dies?'

'O yes,' said Stella, as though a light had dawned on her, 'of course, there must be a heaven for people like that to go to.'

'There's a nightclub on the High Street,' John said changing the subject. 'It's a bit of a dive. They have a floorshow and it gets a bit rowdy sometimes. They're looking for someone to keep order. It's a pound a night. Seven till midnight. If I want the job I can have it.'

'It must be dangerous,' she said, staring into the fire, 'Are you going to do it?'

'When we get our own place, maybe. They have card games there after hours. I think it's illegal. A game called poker.'

'You're good at cards, will you play?' she wanted to know.

'Nah!' he said, 'not me. I don't like gambling. I lost ten bob once on a silly horse! That was enough for me!'

Their little tower of blazing wood had collapsed in the grate; it was powdery grey now that the bright, living glow had gone. It reminded him of those smouldering buildings, demolished by bombs during the war, which they'd pass on their way to church as children. It was like a scene from some other life entirely. Something which made your heart ache because you'd lost the way, and you never would catch up now. That's why you were here, staring at the smouldering wreckage of the fire, because that's what you'd always kept choosing.

'What are you thinking?' Stella asked

'I'm thinking, if I take that bruiser's job, it'll be another seven quid a week.'

'But it's not worth it! It's only four shillings an hour. You could be stabbed, or slashed or something.'

'Feel that,' he said, grinning and flexing his biceps. 'I can take care of myself. Besides, it won't be for long. Just till we get the children down here.'

She was tired. Too tired to argue. She fell asleep. Around midnight two or three of the neighbours came bumping up the bare wooden staircase. There was a burp and a loud hiccup, followed by wheezy giggling and a voice saying, 'Sh! There's a lady in there!'

They were just outside the door. There was a rude remark, a short concert of spluttering laughter and then somehow someone missed his footing and went down with a crash and a curse. John slipped out of bed and stood, fists clenched at the door. He was shivering with fear but they went away. Stella slept on. Someone started singing in the street down below. Just some drunk, but it brought a lump to his throat.

The words went something like . . .
'Let's hang on to what we've got!
Don't let go, 'cause you've got the lot!
Got a lot of love between you,
Hang on! Hang on! Hang on! To what you've got!'

It was the latest hit. John looked across at his wife. A street light filled the room with shadows, but he could see her all right. She seemed totally abandoned to sleep, like a child in a cot. They were on the verge of a new life: a life more volatile and precarious than anything they'd ever known.

John stood in a lay-by on a deserted roadway, watching the sunrise. It was a late spring morning and wreaths of mist were rising from the fields. His trouser pockets were bulging with banknotes. The sun sparkled on his car. It was a dream come true – the Aston Martin he'd always coveted. It was his — bought and paid for. He hadn't had time yet to count the money he had just won. Some of it had been other men's wages – weak foolish men, who had earned their pay fairly enough, but who couldn't help themselves – men with wives and little children. John thought back to those hungry, desperate and yet tender days when Stella and he had clung together in the freezing dark of that caravan, dreaming of a lavish future, which inevitably included an Aston

Martin and plenty of spending money. Well, there was
the car, in all its splendour. Only it seemed to be mocking him. It posed an obvious and embarrassing question:
'Are you happy now?' He would have sworn a man in
his position would feel pretty good. But it wasn't so.
Although he had achieved more than he could ever real-
istically have hoped for, he could feel that familiar lump,
rising in his chest. It was all his mother's fault. It was as
though he couldn't shake her off. He had left the poker
table early. On the way home he was stupid enough to
start humming the tune of a hymn. It was one of his
father's favourites. Then he found himself singing the
words: 'He left His Father's throne above; so free, so infi-
nite His grace; emptied Himself of all but love; and bled
for Adam's helpless race.'

The next thing he knew was that he had to get out
of the car. It was as if something was trying to get him!
'I want to be free!' He shouted out at the top of his
voice. The word 'free' was almost a scream of desperation.

The first time he had walked into a nightclub it
seemed so heady and exciting; he could still smell the
cigar smoke and hear the jukebox.

'One, two three – falling in love with you was easy for
me!' That's the very song that had been playing. This
was it, he thought. This was the life. This was where he
belonged. He was employed as a peacekeeper, so people
naturally expected him to be tough. That was half the
battle. After hours, at about 2 a.m. a poker game would
start; John watched, fascinated by it all. One night he sat
in on a game, and that was the beginning. At first he
loved it. As he absorbed the game, people would tell
him how good he was. They began to ask his opinions
about certain aspects of particular situations they'd
found themselves in. John realised that he had intuition

and concentration. He began to win steadily. The children had come down from Scotland, so the family rented a four-bedroomed house. They bought a brand new car. John wanted his wife and family to have anything they wanted. Christmases, from then on, were lavish affairs. He started work in a casino, dealing cards until two in the morning.

Then the poker game would begin. That's when the serious money was made, or lost. Most days, John liked to go trout fishing, something he had always enjoyed, but it was becoming an obsession. It was a way of escape – something to live for. He would turn up at the fishing lodge in all sorts of exotic cars! He had an image to live up to. Half the fun in life was trying to make people envy him, or so he thought.

Stella began to fret about John. It wasn't enough to have plenty of spending money. Sometimes he would be gone for two or three days and then come home half-dead, wheezing and coughing; too many cigarettes – he couldn't sleep, so he would go off fishing and spend all day lying in the bottom of a boat. The tension began to affect her. Over the years he had tried various ways and means of earning money, but he soon got fed up with them. There'd been a spell of buying and selling vintage cars. John would scour Scotland searching for them, to sell on again in the South. It became too demanding. Eventually he went back to poker. That was the nearest thing he knew to freedom.

But their marriage was suffering; they seemed to be living separate lives. Stella was drinking more and more. Any suggestion that she should ease up would make her throw a tantrum.

'Just leave me alone!' she'd shout. 'Do I tell you how to spend your money? Besides, what else is there? What's this life for? You tell me that. I like drink. I enjoy it. If you can suggest something better, just let me know.'

Where had it all gone wrong? Where was the bliss they had promised themselves? John hated the poker game now, but he couldn't seem to escape it. It was a burden he must carry in order to maintain the illusion of freedom. But he felt trapped. The very thing which was supposed to set him free, had imprisoned him. Bible verses from his past spilled out into his thoughts. The trouble with real Christianity is that it's all or nothing. It was about 5.30 a.m. and his mother would be awake for sure. If birds were singing, he didn't hear them. 'Are you somewhere near?' John said aloud. 'If only You would answer; I'd believe!'

'We hid as it were our faces from him; he was despised and we esteemed him not. Surely he hath borne our griefs, and carried our sorrows . . .' The words came tumbling out, as though he had to get it over and done with. 'But he was wounded for our transgressions, he was bruised for our iniquities; the chastisement of our peace was upon him; and with his stripes we are healed' (Is. 53). The sense of God's love and His presence was almost unbearable. His chest seemed to be swelling up. His eyes were blurred. 'And he made his grave with the wicked,' he said 'and with the rich in his death.' John turned to look at his car; it was like a dark purple blob. Suddenly he felt like just walking off and leaving it.

'I've got to get a grip of myself,' he thought. Wiping his eyes, he began to breathe, deliberately and deeply, arranging the money more evenly in his pockets.

'If Stella ever sees me in a state like this, she'll think I've gone nuts,' he said to himself. He reached for his cigarettes; after a few deep puffs he started laughing.

I suppose there's no heart harder than the heart of a poker professional. And yet it was this very hardness which demonstrated the power of the persistent prayers of a godly mother. In spite of his arrogant bravado, something had happened. Something quite unthinkable: the Aston Martin had lost its lustre. He had to admit that his dream car wasn't the answer. At first he blamed the weather. Summer was coming, so he needed a convertible. The Aston Martin was locked away in a garage, so he bought a two-seater roadster. Now and then, about every eight or ten weeks, John would go to look at the Aston, wondering why he couldn't recapture that first thrill of adoration. Like all idols, it was hopelessly fallible. In the end, after one of those lean periods, that are a permanent hazard to a professional gambler, the car was sold.

Stella was changing. There was a desperation about her. She saw that her life was slipping away. She wanted to be out on the town all the time, drinking and dancing the nights away. The children loved her and confided in her. They all ran wild together. But they seemed afraid and suspicious of John. Stella knew, but they never discussed it. It seemed that life had passed them by and that it was too late for them. She was drifting away from him, just at the very time when he was learning something of what love really was. She was getting her own back, she said, for all the anguish he had caused her in the past.

But something very strange was happening – time after time, John found himself reciting passages of Scripture that he had learned as a boy.

One beautiful summer day, he was still in bed, quite unable to sleep, though utterly exhausted. Outside, he could hear children shouting and laughing as they played together. You could sense their excitement as they chased one another in some game, with never a thought of what this life might do to them. He felt like a prizefighter that has taken too many punches. It was hard to breathe because his chest really did feel like molten lead. Too many cigarettes, but what could you do when the pressure built up? It had been the coughing which had wakened him. The trouble was, he had only been asleep for half an hour. There had been a long, long poker session. As a result, he was deadbeat. There were also terrible headaches, of course, that were the results of years of endless tension and interminable hours of concentration.

John thought about the conversation at the end of the game.

'Remember the old days? Those days when you'd come riding into town in a flashy car and drive off when you'd taken our money. We thought you were a hero. In fact we more or less idolised you. We used to think you were the best we'd ever seen.'

'So what about now?' he'd asked.

'Nah!' said the gambler. 'We don't fear you any more. You're gone – cracked up. It happens to everyone in the end. Take last night for instance. You made a mistake you'd never have made once. It cost you everything.'

It was true. John was worn and tired. He couldn't take any more. He had to get up, because there'd be no peace or sleep for him that day. 'No peace,' says God, 'for the wicked.'

That verse had always raised a laugh because of the defiant bravado in his voice, but he could see the irrefutable truth of it. He decided to have a lukewarm bath. Perhaps that would cool him down and wash away the weariness and the bad form, as gamblers say. As the water was running John caught sight of himself in the mirror; he caught a glimpse of some complete stranger. Moving closer, he stared at the ghastly image.

The skin of his face looked like putty. His eyes were dark and bloodshot.

'What are you?' he asked himself. 'Are you dead, or dying, or just killing yourself?'

'There is a way that seems right to a man,' came the reply, 'but in the end it leads to death.'

Why did God's word keep coming back to him?

As he sat on the bath, a wave of self-pity over-whelmed him. He realised now that there wasn't a shred of genuine repentance in him: never had been. The only thing that concerned him was his injured pride and the loss of his reputation. He knew several washed-out gamblers, fellows who had once posed, strutted and been admired and respected by 'lesser' men. He didn't want to end up like them – furtive fellows who bored everyone with wildly exaggerated stories about past glories. But he was like them. He had been going downhill for a long time. It was all far too much of a struggle. It was time to call it a day.

John unlocked the bathroom door and went to find Stella.

'I'm finished,' he told her. 'It's over. It's just not me anymore. I've played my last hand of poker.'

'What are we going to do now?' she asked brightly. She didn't mind. Anything was all right by her. John looked at her with deep gratitude. They had been through so much together. Most other women, he thought, would have left him for good, long ago.

John, by now, was forty-five years old. He decided he would start a business. Both he and Stella began to get excited. His gambling friend, of many years, John the Greek, was more sceptical. He ran a game at home and together they had been in some tough situations. He would have cheated John Searle if he got the chance, but it worked both ways. Nevertheless, he was the closest thing to a friend a gambler can have.

'See you tomorrow night. We're starting a bit early. The Bedford boys are coming,' John the Greek informed him over the phone. 'Don't be late, your friend Mark's flying over from Germany for the game.'

'I won't be there, John,' insisted John S. 'I told you, I've given it up. I'm going to make my fortune and retire.'

'Suit yourself but I don't believe you. You're like me. I'll die a gambler. I've lived a gambler and that's what I'll be when I die, and so will you.'

Starting a new business didn't seem to pose any problems to John, who was well used to running risks. A disused Victorian Sunday school in a back street cul-de-sac next to a scrap yard came to his attention. It was a vast, unheated hall in a shocking state of neglect, but he caught the vision of an emporium that would sell anything old.

'We're antique dealers!' he announced to Stella.

'Hurrah!' she laughed. 'That sounds good. What do we know about antiques?'

'Not much, nothing, really, but then if you know everything, you'll never learn!'

They compensated for their ignorance by sheer hard work and plenty of bluff. The business flourished and they loved it. Before dawn, John would be up restoring furniture that had been abused or neglected. Together, they scoured the salesrooms for bargains. But something was happening to Stella, which made her dissatisfied, restless and was beyond explanation. One day, in the normal course of conversation, John blasphemed using the name of Christ to express disgust.

'Don't say that!' she warned. 'Don't say it ever again! I hate you saying that! Say anything else you want!

Anything! I don't care! But don't abuse the name of Jesus Christ!'

Unknown to John, for some months she had been feeling an occasional compulsion to find a quiet place, perhaps on a park bench by the river, where she would try to pray. Not that she knew how, or why.

'Our Father,' she whispered, 'Hallowed be Thy name, forgive us our debts, as we forgive . . .' and that was about all she knew. She didn't even realise that the prayer was in the Bible. Sometimes she could hardly wait to be alone so that she could try to commune with God somehow. Not that she suddenly became some kind of saint! In fact she began to drink very heavily.

One time she came back from an auction with three ancient Bibles. One of them was too large to be convenient. They couldn't sell it, so Stella decided to keep it. It was a massive tome with the history of a local village family, hand-written in a special section between the two Testaments. It dated back to 1829. There were dozens of old books in their shop, but when Stella was alone, she was irresistibly drawn to read the Bible. As she searched through the pages, she came across an engraving of the crucifixion. She sat staring at it for a long time. Gradually, the shocking reality of it seemed to dawn on her.

'Why?' the question demanded an answer. 'Why did they do it?'

She read the chapter on the opposite page – it was John 19. It made her indignant. She had only ever prayed in tense and desperate personal circumstances, but she reckoned that her prayers had certainly been answered. If Jesus was so kind and so powerful, why did those men abuse Him so wickedly and why did He just let them do it? What did that horrible word 'scourge' mean? She imagined poor Mary, standing by helplessly. She thought of her own sons and wondered how she would feel.

Stella never dared ask John to answer her questions, probably because she feared he would sneer and scoff at her, so she resolved to go to church. All the family had a bit of a laugh at her, as she 'dressed up' to go. Unfortunately, although she attended for more than a year she didn't really understand anything. Her enthusiasm began to wane. She was disappointed. John used to tell her off for going to the evening service three-parts drunk!

The property boom, which swept south-east England in the 1980s, had just begun. People, who became millionaires almost overnight, would find themselves dispossessed and swamped with debts when the market crashed. Stella jumped on the bandwagon too. Arriving home to find a 'For Sale' sign planted in the front garden, John discovered that an agent had been invited to sell their house. John uprooted the sign and hurled it into some bushes, but when they were offered a huge profit on the original price, he gave in.

They had looked casually at a large, imposing Victorian house in desperate need of renovation. Stella, who was always more a gambler than her husband, decided to buy it.

The new house was foul with damp, so a local firm was called in to survey the situation.

'As I spoke to their representative, I had an unmistakable conviction that the man was a Christian. I'd been cursing and blaspheming as he looked around the house, but he never gave any sign or hint of disapproval, and yet somehow I felt compelled to stop swearing. I sensed in him that Spirit of power, love and self-discipline that I had seen in other Christians. Some time later, I heard a voice on a local radio programme, a voice I'd heard somewhere before. It was the surveyor; he was sharing his life story about how he had become a Christian. It was simple, strong, and sound. I held my breath, listening; then I shouted, "Stella, Stella, come quickly!" We listened as the interview came to a close. He'd only been a Christian a couple of years.'

'So what are the advantages of your new-found faith?' the interviewer asked. 'Well,' said the man, 'I just couldn't imagine life without Jesus Christ any more.'

'That,' said the interviewer, 'was Ben Hicks.'

John felt compelled to talk to him again. Ben and his wife were to become firm friends of the Searles. They were to be like signposts, pointing the family to Jesus Christ.

But meanwhile, they were still caught up in dreams of untold wealth, which seemed to be materialising before their eyes. The new house was gaining in value so quickly they couldn't get used to it. John would daydream about having enough to retire, with no more worries. They would live near the sea and laze away their days doing exactly as they pleased. The only trouble was that, unknown to John, the thought of such a life horrified Stella. It sounded like a living death to her. It was impossible to ignore the fact that alcohol was becoming a serious problem. She wanted freedom to indulge her obsession without any restrictions.

'But darling, can't you see that you're going to kill yourself?' John pleaded.

'So what! Don't "darling" me. What do you care? Besides, it's my business. If I want to kill myself I will, but I'm at least going to have some fun while I'm doing it!'

John couldn't take it in as never before had she been so cynical and disillusioned. Just when it seemed that their 'ship was coming in' at last, alcohol had become the first consideration of her life and it was destroying their relationship.

'Can't you get it through your head,' she said one day, 'that no one actually loves you? I don't, and neither do the children. In fact they can't stand you. Do they ever confide in you? No. You're an ogre that's why. The minute Angela's married and gone, I'm off too. I'm going to drink myself to death and good riddance.'

That was drink talking!

The next day they would carry on normally, as though no such bitter things had been said. John felt that it was like living with two people.

One fateful day he met a gambling acquaintance from the past. Three years had elapsed since he last sat at a poker table.

'Have you heard about John the Greek? He's in hospital. Here's the ward number.'

'Surely I'll go' John Searle promised. 'I'd love to cheer him up. What's wrong with him anyway?'

'He's dying,' the man said, 'It's terminal.'

'Sorry. Count me out. That's just too heavy for me. I don't like hospitals at the best of times, but death gives me the jitters.'

'What kind of man are you?' He looked disgusted. 'Have you no respect? John the Greek likes you. He thinks you're his friend. He needs all his friends just now.'

When John told Stella about the conversation her immediate response was one of compassion.

'O, the poor man, you must go and visit him,' she said.

It was true that John S. had shared so much of his life with his friend, who had been a frequent visitor to the family house.

But for the last two or three years John S. had avoided him, because all he ever talked about was his daughter. Her mother had left him, taking his little girl away. All his money had been spent on solicitors, trying to win custody. He became obsessed. The court ordered him to stop harassing his daughter and her mother. He ended up in prison because he smashed open the door where his daughter lived.

Looking bewildered and diminished, he told John S., 'I only wanted to see my little girl.'

Perhaps he wasn't so tough after all. And now he was dying.

Two weeks later, John went to see him. He vividly remembers the encounter:

'Hospitals used to really give me the creeps. I felt apprehensive as the silent, automatic doors opened and then closed behind me. It was as if I'd been swallowed up. How many poor souls had passed away last week alone, in this vast complex of hushed corridors and side wards, with their fearful terminal secrets? That's the sort of thing I was wondering about as I looked for my old gambling companion. How would he look? Would he be hooked up to those bottles and tubes, imprisoned by the ghastly impedimenta, which seemed to be the trappings of serious illness?

'It was a relief to find him in a day room, watching television. He was wearing a snow-white dressing gown. There was a "No Smoking" sign on the wall, but John the Greek had a cigarette in his mouth.

'"Hey! Can't you read English yet?"' John pointed at the sign.

'He grinned. "What are they going to do?" he said, "Shoot me?" He took out another fag and lit it with the stub of the one he'd just finished. "Did you know that smoking can kill you?" he went on, his eye glinting with wicked humour. "Here, take a chance," he said, offering the packet "You have one."'

John remembers, 'We both laughed as I lit up. He began talking. The conversation was all about poker, about the schemes and the fiddles and the dangers and disappointments we'd shared in the old days. This wasn't so bad, I was thinking, but suddenly my friend began to name names of heavy gamblers we'd known, young men who had lived at breakneck speed and who had died suddenly from heart seizure.

'"Where are they?" my friend asked, "Will I see them soon?" I shrugged without answering.

'"Tell you what I think," he went on, "There's going to be a big poker game in the sky – the greatest game there ever was. I'll be sitting in soon, and there'll be a seat for you some day."

'That was his concept of heaven. He was making a terrific effort to sound carefree and jovial, but I could see right through him. He never lacked courage and he had always been a great bluffer, but he couldn't bluff me. I knew him far too well. All the signs were there. Inside, he was tense with fear. He lit his fourth cigarette from the butt of the third, concentrating hard on what he was doing. His face suddenly clouded over.

'"I wonder if my little girl's going to get to come and see me," he said. He pronounced it "Liddel gel." I looked away; I just couldn't bear to see his face. We sat there, terribly quiet, each knowing what the other was thinking.

'This was the end of this life for him and he desperately wanted to know what was next. As far as he was concerned, I was the one who could set his mind at rest.

'"Things don't look too good for me," he said at last. "I'm finding this a bit hard." Another awkward silence. "Too many nights without sleep," he continued. "Too many cigarettes. Too much drinking and heavy gambling. We've lived a wild, hard life and we have to pay for it. That's only fair, and I'm not complaining. We called the tune, and now we have to pay the piper, so you tell me, Johnny, what do I owe him? What does he want from me? There must be something, I have to know."

"'Don't start worrying about all that rubbish," I snapped. "You've enough to cope with, without driving yourself nuts."

'He wasn't satisfied. "'I had a word with the surgeon yesterday," he told me. "He says that if he operates, there's not much chance of me coming out of the theatre alive. If he doesn't operate I've maybe got six months. What do you think I should do?"

"'Look, man," I said fiercely, "I'm no doctor! Leave me alone! What do I know? I'm not God!" I was in turmoil now. Oughtn't I be trying to comfort and encourage my friend? "What's the matter with you?" I was saying to myself. "Why don't you give the poor man some hope? Tell him the doctors make mistakes. Tell him that miracles sometimes happen. Remind him of those spectacular long shots he's played in the past. While there's life there's hope after all!"

'And then I saw a plain and clear truth, which was the beginning of the fundamental change in my life. It was as if the truth answered my own questions.

"'What hope is there for your friend? If he were to make a miraculous recovery, and prove all the doctors wrong – if he were to walk out of here and go back to the poker table and dog track and the bookmaker's shop – if he were to carry on pining for his daughter for another five years, or ten, or twenty, what hope is that? There's no real hope for him. No such thing, because the surest bet in all the world is that one day he'd certainly have to face the dilemma he's facing now. Can't you see that he has no hope?"

'I could see it. I saw it more clearly than I'd ever seen anything. I watched him lighting another cigarette. "You're dead my friend," I said to myself. "And so are you," said the voice of truth. I couldn't cope of course. I just wanted to be out of there, to run away, to escape. I stood up and held out my hand. My friend took it, and then put his arms around me. The façade fell way, the bluff was over. We couldn't pretend any more. The game was up, as this was a matter more important than life or death. I couldn't say anything. I just held him in my arms as you would a friend who's going on a journey, which is so dangerous you don't expect to see him again. Underneath his loose, white dressing gown, he was all skin and bone, like a bag of dried sticks. I stood away. We looked at each other for a moment. It was as if he had this one last really important question to ask me. He'd heard me quote Scripture and pray mocking prayers. He knew my background. Surely there was something I could tell him.

'"Goodbye John," I said, "I'll come and see you again some time."

'"I know," he answered, "I know you will. Thanks for coming, anyway."

'It was his way of saying that he knew we'd never meet again.'

John Searle walked down the long corridor as quickly as he decently could. When he reached the end, he turned to wave goodbye. John the Greek seemed so far away, a shrunken, round-shouldered figure in a small doorway at the end of a long, shiny tunnel. He lifted one hand, looking exactly like some little child in a class who's feeling very sick and who wants to leave the room.

Once outside, John Searle was angry with him, with himself and with the whole 'stupid' world.

'So what!' he said to himself. 'People die every second! Besides, what could you do? He's had a good life. Did as he pleased. Lived the life of a gambler, and that's how he said he'd die. Let him get on with it! He wouldn't ever listen to sense anyway. Always getting involved in situations he couldn't handle.'

John turned his back on his friend and went trout fishing.

A few months later he met the man who had first told him that his friend was ill. 'I went to visit him. He was very upset. How is he now, by the way?'

'He's dead,' said the man. 'Didn't you know? He's been dead for weeks.'

John Searle ran home to tell Stella. Hoisting up their little terrier dog under one arm, John announced that he was off out for a walk.

He drove out of town, parked the car, and crossed a stile. It was the place where he used to walk his racing greyhounds.

It was springtime. The hedgerows looked as if they were hung with pure, white lace, as the blackthorn bushes were in blossom. Standing beneath a cloudless sky, John felt that the whole earth seemed to be brimming with the excitement of new life. But all seemed pointless and futile. While the birds twittered and lambs chased one another in the fields, he felt as if something was missing from the landscape, as if some familiar tree had been struck down in a storm. He stopped and looked up at the empty sky.

'John's dead!' he cried, 'John's dead!'

In the next few moments, words poured into his mind – words he had learned as a child, from the Bible. Their power came as a shock to him.

'Jesus said, "I am the resurrection and the life. He who believes in me will live even though he dies; and whoever lives and believes in me will never die"' (John 11:25).

John felt afraid. Looking round, he saw and heard nothing and yet this tremendous verse had 'exploded' and pierced him with revelation of dynamic truth, which made undeniable sense. John called the dog, picked him up and fled from the place. As he drove home, more words flooded back . . . and touched his heart.

"'I am the living bread that came down from heaven. If anyone eats of this bread he will live forever. This bread is my flesh, which I give for the life of the world"' (John 6:51).

"'I tell you the truth, a time is coming and has now come when the dead will hear the voice of the Son of God and those who hear will live"' (John 5:25).

His will, however, refused to surrender. One part of him longed to submit to the Lordship and control of Christ, but there were deep-seated fears and doubts and an inborn rebellion against that one hundred percent commitment, which he kne, was the only true door to real Christianity. Six months or so passed. Things didn't become easier, in fact, he felt that each day the burden he was carrying, seemed to grow heavier. He couldn't work properly, and sometimes felt so dark and despairing that he would hardly utter a word.

'I remember hiding in the back bedroom, looking out over the garden, filling my mind with curses in order to keep at bay all thoughts of God's redeeming love in Christ. What would my wife and family think of me if I turned into a religious crank? Besides, I'd been through it all before. I wouldn't be able to keep it up – I knew that well enough.'

One day an old neighbour came to visit. He told them that his son have been converted to Christ and baptised. 'You should see him now, he's absolutely transformed,' he said.

John was incredulous. The son had been one of those people to avoid if possible. His whole life had been in constant turmoil. John scoffed and sneered but, when he was told the name of the church where this had happened, he decided to have a look for himself. One Sunday, John rose early, bathed and put on a suit. The family stared open-mouthed when he explained that he was going to church!

Handing out the hymnbooks in the foyer, and shaking hands with folk as they filed in, was the neighbour's son. He was wearing a white pullover and blue jeans and trainers.

'Does he realise what a soppy jerk he looks?' John said to himself. 'Poor twit. Doesn't he even realise he should be wearing his best suit?'

'Whatever are you doing here?' the young man gasped.

'That's a nice welcome – can't I come in? Didn't you know that church isn't for Holy Joes? It's for sinners!'

Martin Travers, the minister must have preached his heart out. John, who could tell a mile off that he was utterly sincere, couldn't forget something he said.

'Even if you've spent years running away from God, He still loves you. Even if you've ignored or insulted Him by turning your back on Him, He still loves you and longs for you to know Him.'

John Searle, the gambler and blasphemer, stopped running.

He took God at His word.

He turned and asked Jesus Christ to forgive all his sins and come to live in his heart. The burden he had been carrying for so long was lifted, never to return, for Christ had died, paying the punishment for all John's sin.

The first few months of his new life, in Christ, were filled with mixed emotions and reactions. Friends told

him that it was all a flash in the pan. They had seen it all
before, of course, and thought that he would get over it.
John, himself, wondered if he could keep it up. He
would have a few sleepless nights (during which he
prayed for hours on end telling God how weak he felt
and asking God to help him), before he discovered that
there is nothing we can do at all. It is Christ and He
alone who keeps us.

'Now it is God who makes both us and you stand firm
in Christ. He anointed us, set His seal of ownership on
us, and put His spirit in our hearts as a deposit, guaran-
teeing what is to come!' (2 Cor. 1:21,22).

From that day onward, John never feared for his
future as a believing Christian.

After all the dashed hopes, the heartaches and
ruinous disappointments of a faithless, loveless life of
sin, he now knows the power of God's grace – grace to
save and grace to keep.

John Searle, ex-gambler, has exchanged his wild life to
become a pastor of a church. He still travels, but now
includes journeys to Malawi where he helped to found
an orphanage. Working alongside the churches out there
and with the support of others back home, John has been
instrumental in establishing an organic farm, making
boreholes to provide clean water as well as supplying
Bibles.

'The children come with sores, worms and gummed-
up eyes, but now they are nourished and well-cared for
– they are beautiful.'

By the way, he still has that little Bible, that somehow
never got lost or sold, which his mother packed in his
bag when he went into the army. On the flyleaf, along
with some verses of Scripture, is an inscription in his
mother's handwriting.

'John, constant love and prayers, mother and dad.'

Stella, meanwhile, had become fascinated with the words of Scripture for herself. While John was in the workshop, Stella would write quoting great chunks of the Bible to their son Paul, who was in prison for fraud. He must have wondered what on earth was going on with his mother!

One day her eyes lighted on an engraving of the cross. Gazing at it she wondered, 'What's it all about?' As she read the words in John 19 and 20 she thought about Mary at the foot of the cross watching her son being punished. Stella readily identified with the mother, as Stella's own son was in prison – only Paul was guilty whereas Jesus was innocent. What had Mary felt? What did it mean to her? Stella wondered about all these things in her heart.

Once, when she was passing a church noticeboard, Stella read a big sign. It announced, 'CH-CH What's missing?'

Stella looked again but didn't understand. Back at home she asked John if he knew.

'CH UR CH – What's missing, why UR – you are!' he explained.

Stella chose to start going to church, although at times she was half drunk.

After John was converted and despite his explanations, Stella would often say, 'Nothing like that has happened to me.'

It seemed that nothing was getting through to Stella.

One morning she was late getting out of bed; this was not unusual for she often had a hangover. John went to his own church, but Stella made her way to a different one in Cambridge, which had two services. She made it in time for the later one. John, having finished at his church, headed over to meet Stella. Creeping in at the back he looked through a glass partition to see if he

could spot his wife. There she was, sitting at the front.
The preacher was just launching into his sermon.

'I hope he doesn't use long words,' thought John, 'just
keep it simple for Stella.'

He knew that this church attracted quite a few
'eggheads and clever dicks' as he called them, from the
university. But there in among them all was his Stella,
who at primary school had taken two hours to learn the
word 'because'.

The speaker was preaching about the parable of the
tenants from Luke's gospel, where the phrase comes,
'When the tenants saw him, they talked the matter over.'
He went on to explain that whenever and wherever the
good news about Jesus is preached, that is what happens
– people talk the matter over. When the service ended,
everyone left their seats to queue for the free coffee.
Stella, however, remained sitting at the front, open-
mouthed. John made his way over to her. She told him,
'John, I've seen it all!' At last she understood the message of the gospel that 'God so loved the world that He
sent his one and only Son that whoever believes in Him
should not perish but have everlasting life.'

Their lives changed, as their desire was now to live
lives pleasing to God, rather than living like a bunch of
crooks! One by one the children and their spouses
became Christians – utterly transformed by the gospel.

Stella, armed with a bicycle and a shopping basket
began selling mineral water to local residents. Slowly,
custom built up and the business expanded, but she has
always managed to give a percentage to the charity,
Aquaid, set up to bring aid directly to the Third World.

Her tenacity is something her husband is proud of.
Together, they now work devoting themselves to God
and others, in order to bring relief and spiritual help to
hundreds of starving children in the continent of Africa.

John's mother, who is still alive, always felt that one of her sons would return to Africa one day; but perhaps she didn't reckon on it being John – the boy who used to put fireworks through their local mission hall letter box, but who returned in later years to preach in the very same hall as a new person in Christ.

*Adapted with permission from The *Presbyterian Herald*.

7. THE BUSINESSMAN

Bill Capper

Making money in the place where money is made could well describe Bill Capper. His home is found near the Royal Mint in South Wales. Bill is a businessman employing seven hundred people in both the wholesale business and the chain of shops he runs. Supporting nearly five hundred stores from South Wales to the south east of England, the annual turnover is in excess of £200 million.

At the beginning of the twentieth century, before the days of supermarkets, hypermarkets, trolleys and check-outs, Bill's grandfather started in business as a whole-sale grocer in Newport, Monmouthshire. He set a high standard of integrity in business dealing. Soon he earned the respect of a growing number of shopkeepers in the area. Today the business is still a family concern (quite rare these days), supplying Spar neighbourhood stores, opening long hours.

Llantrisant in South Wales, where Bill's family live, once famously provided archers for the battle of Crecy in 1346. The local inhabitants of this day and age, are no longer required for such duties – they are more interested in meeting targets of a very different kind!

Flick through the business pages of any newspaper and you will be confronted by headlines such as: 'Five hundred job losses' and 'Rising oil prices push RPI to all-time high' and 'First half profits doubled'.

With pressure to meet deadlines, pay wages, make profits and still keep sane how does Bill view life? Do God and mammon fit comfortably in his worldview? Some of the values Bill expresses were passed down through his family who were to have a big influence on him in later years.

'I was number two in our family of six brothers and sisters. My memories of home are very happy ones. From early on I was introduced to the business. The aromas of the bacon-smoking room, the packing of flour and cereals, imported dried fruit and the cooking of hams, left a lasting impression. A childhood memory, from about the age of seven, is going to the warehouse at night to look for rats with my father. My job was to turn on the lights when we heard a rat so that he could shoot it!

'The summer holidays spent in Cornwall were great. My parents, who had a deep Christian faith, always put God first in their lives. Even on holidays we were able to meet up with other Christians, joining in enthusiastically with them in beach activities at Bude. I was well aware that God loved me. I was only six years old when I first made a response, in my heart, to the love of God. I don't recall much about it. It was only later that I really understood the full implications of following Christ. It is very reassuring that God does not expect us to become learned theologians to qualify to belong to his family. Loving God during early childhood may prevent a life being wasted in harmful or selfish ways.

'Leaving the family home, for the first time, at the age of nine I went away to boarding school in Derbyshire. I remember learning to swim in the river Dove, and catching sticklebacks in a jam jar with a piece of bread and some string. When I was twelve, a teacher came to the school who made a deep impression on me. He had an infectious enthusiasm for everything he did and a great love for God. He was speaking to us one Sunday afternoon on the Bible verse, God 'now commands all men everywhere to repent' (Acts 17:30). I had never thought of it so personally before. I certainly knew there was plenty of wrong in my life as far as God was concerned and it weighed heavily on me. The teacher told us how we could turn from our wrong ways and ask God for forgiveness in a prayer, but it was only later during the next holidays that I realised God had answered me.

'I was reading the book *Conscience*, by Professor Hallesby, in which he describes how the Holy Spirit of God brings about in us a deep sense that we are in the wrong before a holy God. He then explains how this guilt is lifted when we repent and put our faith in Jesus Christ for forgiveness of our sins and also how the Holy Spirit comes to live in the new Christian. I suddenly realised that this was just what had happened to me. From that time on, God gave me the assurance that I was one of His children.

'I went to public school and later university where I joined in with the activities of the Christian Union. One of the most valuable things for life was to learn how reliable the Bible documents are and how they are God's true Word to us today. I began to think about what future career I might follow. I carefully considered whether I should go abroad, as a missionary, but felt God wanted me in ordinary employment. I was offered a job in computing, but it was after university, during a visit to a Spar wholesale business in Austria, that I felt the family business was the place for me.

'After a period of training away from home I started to get involved on the management accounting side; it was not plain sailing and after a few years, I decided that it wasn't for me after all and I started job hunting. I told my father and said things to him, which must have been very hurtful. God had other plans for me however! Our church held its Sunday evening service in a school assembly hall. One day, when I was the chairman and my father was preaching, he suddenly collapsed with a heart attack, dying later that night in hospital.

'The shock made the memory of that time very vivid. I went up to my bedroom and prayed that God would forgive me for the hurtful things I had said, and if it were possible, that He would tell my father that I was sorry, although I would have liked to tell him myself.'

Bill Capper then found himself in charge of the family business at the early age of twenty-five. As he settled into his new role, he found that his father had been very widely respected in the trade for his Christian principles. He had built solid business relationships, which were going to help Bill in his new position. All thought of another career went out of Bill's mind from then on. Through his inexperience he made a lot of mistakes, but with the help of colleagues at work and the inner strength which God supplies, Bill survived those early years.

Bill felt his responsibilities keenly, as he later described, 'Because of the difficulties we were experiencing, I used to grapple with the question whether or not being a Christian guaranteed the survival of the business, let alone whether it would prosper. There were a couple of hundred people whose jobs would be lost if the business floundered. But I came to realise that there is no guarantee that God will make His people prosper. We have to rely on Him for everyday strength and, sometimes, we have to go through adverse circumstances. Yet, there were also promises, that my father had felt God was making him, about the future, which I was to see fulfilled in an unexpected manner.'

First of all however came marriage. A girl from his church really impressed him by becoming captain of the Cambridge hockey team. Later on she won his heart as well and they were married in 1974.

On their honeymoon in Turkey they had an amazing escape.

'Heather and I made the mistake of accepting a lift from two men, who then refused to drop us off at our hotel. They appeared friendly at first but as the afternoon and evening wore on, it seemed they had other ideas. I was glad I had taken a photo of them earlier in the day. I had taken the film out of my camera and put it in my pants in case I should be found dumped in a ditch somewhere! They stopped the car and one of then got in the back wanting to sit next to Heather, but I moved over to sit in the middle! The next time the car stopped, Heather and I made a run for it in the dark, but they caught up with us. Eventually the leader of the pair fell asleep, after drinking a bottle of spirits, and we persuaded the driver to take us back to the hotel. I was very thankful to God for watching over us.'

They settled down into their new home in Newport, eventually starting a family of their own. It was then that Bill was particularly conscious of God's leading in his life. In 1976 business and family life were to change dramatically with a move away from Newport, to the area where they now live. 'I always associate the move with a time when Heather and I particularly set aside time to pray, although a move was the last thing we wanted or expected. The business needed bigger premises to operate from but we could not afford the necessary building programme on a site we had earmarked nearby. In a most remarkable way the opportunity came to buy a warehouse twenty miles away.

'A large chain of grocery stores was shutting down its distribution depot in Talbot Green. The owners were anxious to sell and find employment for their staff if possible. A new manager had come to our bank, who had the confidence of his superiors to an unusual degree. He took a very favourable view of the opportunity to buy the depot and in due course an agreement was reached. Because commercial property prices were depressed, the depot was two and a half times bigger than it would have been possible to build, for the same amount of money! Amazingly the old premises in Newport sold for their full value, so our borrowings were reduced. Within just a few years we had repaid the bank loan completely.'

The rat race, pressure to make profits, to take unfair advantage of others, and to get even with rivals can sour or become a big temptation to businessmen. It can even be the norm.

The Bible has a lot to say to the business world. There is much in it about just dealings, how to treat your staff, fair weights and measures, and attitudes to money for instance. It is surprising how many of the 'latest management techniques' are as old as the hills and found as principles in God's word.

'It has been my experience that Jesus is a reliable friend and the Bible a sure guide for life. One example concerns a company in which our business is a shareholder and of which I am a director. At one time there were strong disagreements about the running of the company, which might seriously affect its future and the future of our family business. I stayed in the hotel where a meeting was due to start next morning and my mind was in turmoil. I woke early and, as is my habit, started to read my Bible and pray. I read how Jesus had calmed the storm on the lake by a word of command. He was Lord of nature and I realised that I too was part of his creation and that He could give me a similar calm as I went into a stormy meeting with so much at stake. He did, and as the day wore on, from time to time I prayed a silent, "Thank you," to Him for being with me.'

A man of integrity, Bill Capper has provided the business world with an example of what honesty and hard work are able to achieve, even in the environment of mammon, thanks in no small way to the Christian faith, which is such a vital part of his experience.

8. THE BRIDGE PLAYER

Jane Scales

An attractive sophisticated lady of middle years settled down to her customary game of bridge. Her companions afforded entertaining conversation and the game, regular amusement. But, through no fault of her friends, this game was to be her last.

The blue skies and vast lands of Kenya provided an almost idyllic start to Jane's life. Brought up on a farm in Kenya, with relatives as neighbours, Jane toddled into a carefree life with enthusiastic abandon. However, before reaching her sixth birthday she suffered a cruel blow: her mother died.

Change was then in the air as her father decided to take her, with her sister, to England. War had been dreadful, but even so Jane's father joined the army.

Jane's arrival in England was postponed because on the way round South Africa, her father dropped them off at a Roman Catholic convent. She was to stay there until the end of the War. Without mother or father and far from the comfort and security of her home, Jane embarked on an education with a religious slant.

She remarks about that time, 'I learned to pray to the saints and how to baptise babies in cases of emergency. I also learned to fear that the devil would appear to me like he had to Saint Theresa!'

Eventually, with the War in Europe ending, Jane's father sent for his two children to return to his new home in England. In those days there was no luxury liner or jumbo jet but simply a troop ship. After final goodbyes, a long journey and boredom at sea, they arrived safety at Southampton. Their father and their new stepmother met them with a ten-month-old sister.

Jane was no stranger to travel and before long she found herself living in vastly different places including the Orkney Isles, Glasgow and Margate. But a return to Kenya eventually came and with it the thought of normality and family life. However, it was not only Europe that was changing politically. There were rumours of the Mau-Mau uprising. (Some blacks had taken an oath to remove the white man from Africa.)

Jane's stepmother disliked living in Kenya so they sold up and moved back to England.

By now, Jane had spent years in different schools, travelled thousands of miles, and encountered family difficulties. Her sister didn't get on with their stepmother, so they ended up living with an aunt and uncle.

'My aunt was an upright, strict person. I found it extremely hard to feel really loved,' Jane sadly admits.

Finally, she had a nervous breakdown; the doctor called it 'extreme melancholia'. An outsider would have found it difficult to understand why.

Jane describes how people viewed her life.

'We lived in a lovely country home and after I qualified as a teacher, I had a good job. I belonged to tennis, badminton and golf clubs where I made lots of friends. I had men friends who were well-off and could afford to take me to big dances and out to dinner.'

Yet Jane was unhappy.

She missed having her own real mother. Not surprisingly, she suffered from feelings of inadequacy. She felt she had no value or worth. Relationships became too difficult to cope with.

Her job as a teacher was proving to be really hard. Then, an offer of marriage came along. She accepted, but it was partly to get away from home and also her job.

Marriage wasn't all it had promised to be. In fact it turned out to be a very lonely marriage which, as her husband was not committed to her, ended in divorce.

Jane moved once more and soon she married again. It is said that 'hurry is of the devil' and so it proved to be. She divorced for the second time.

However, Jane was not on her own now for she had a family – two girls and a boy. 'I would gladly have sunk into the ground. I didn't want to face life any more but because of the children, I carried on. All through the years I cried to God for help and looked for it in all sorts of places. To start with, I thought that by the law of averages life would even up and come right – it didn't! I looked in psychology books but I think they just give you excuses. They certainly didn't give me the answer I wanted.

'I am ashamed to say I even visited a fortune-teller a couple of times but I couldn't take that seriously. Once I went to a hypnotherapist but again I found no answer.'

Did she turn to God?

'Well, I did try reading the Bible, but the words "knock and the door will be opened" were just words. There seemed, to me, at that time to be no real God.'

Just as despair was taking hold, having tried so many things, a simple incident triggered off a series of events, which were to turn her life around.

Walking into the common room one day at school, Jane happened to notice, on the table, a book, which she began to read. It was written by a woman called Joni Eareckson, who related how she coped after becoming a paraplegic, following a diving accident. Subsequently she thanked God for her tragedy because it caused her to seek and find God.

Not long after, Jane was reading an extract from *Readers Digest* about Betsy Ten Boom, a Dutch lady, who was taken to Ravensbruck concentration camp during the Second World War. She was a Christian whose faith affected not only her own personal behaviour, but also influenced many of the inmates. Her ability to trust God in the most awful circumstances, which ultimately ended in her death, made a profound impression on Jane.

Ever an avid reader Jane readily devoured other books loaned to her by the owner of the Joni Eareckson book. A friendship developed along with an awareness that here was the answe: God was real. However, she still did know Him in a personal way.

'Then I listened to a tape about the crucifixion and all that the Lord endured. At the end I was in tears. I began wondering how something I'd known about for years, was relevant to me. I'd attended Anglican churches, read the Common Prayer book, sung hymns and even been confirmed – so what was I to do? I'd even taught my children to say prayers at night and sent them to church to be confirmed. Listening to that tape gave me a sense of my own wrongdoing – being responsible for Christ's death. I realised all that the Lord had done for me. All my sins had been laid on the cross. He paid the punishment for them, in my place, so that I might be forgiven. By then I was in tears. God was real and He had done a wonderful thing in my life. I was so thankful.

My two daughters, at around about the same time and quite independently, were also converted by God.

The family's reaction to all this was mixed. Of course, her two daughters were delighted. She was out of favour with her stepmother, however, who did not approve of Jane's new beliefs or for her telling her father. She started praying for the rest of the family to know about the God who cares for and loves them.

Church was no longer a chore. She actually enjoyed going – not once but even twice on Sundays! She had always loved reading but it was the Bible that really got her attention: it made her sit up and think. Now she knew the Author, it was beginning to make sense.

'I used to be mad keen on sport. I loved golf, tennis, and squash passionately. In fact, I once could have said I didn't know how I could live without them.' Sport, which had been like a god to her, didn't have the same hold on her as it once had and the desire for playing bridge simply faded away into her past.

Jane found that God had done a radical work in her life, regenerating it from a careless, unbelieving, dissatisfied one – to a life of peace, security and eternal hope.

She used to view her life as a game of uncertainty, involving trivial pursuits for personal gain; Jane now regards life far more positively, as an adventure with her God.

9. THE ATHLETE

Barrington Williams

The hot sun beat down on the silvery sand. Palm trees swayed gently in the breeze.

The glorious blue sea edged its way gradually up the beach.

This was Jamaica in the fifties.

Somewhere in the beautiful hilly area of central Jamaica, a tiny baby cried; Chester Barrington Williams had just been born.

What would become of this child?

Would he grow up to be a storekeeper, a farmer or perhaps a fisherman? The prospects didn't look too good. For one thing, he was a sickly child; his parents did not expect him to live. For the first eight years of his life his grandmother brought him up. In fact, for a time, he thought that his grandmother was his real mother. His parents, like so many other Jamaicans of that era, had emigrated to England in order to earn more money to provide for their family. In 1963, however, it was time to be reunited with his parents. For Barrington, this was the saddest time of his life for he had to say his final goodbyes to his grandmother. He was never to see her again; she died in 1980.

Barrington and his brother, who was three years older, boarded their plane on 13 October 1963. He had gone down with food poisoning and during the whole of the flight he was sick – leaving a terrible mess on the floor! Apparently, his grandmother had asked a lady to look after them both during the journey. Once they had entered the plane, she was never seen again!

On arrival in England, Barrington was introduced, for the first time, to his parents. It must have been difficult for them all. He soon found out about fog, rain, cold summers and cold winters! Barrington had started on a learning curve, as he began to experience English culture.

'In Great Britain there seemed to be plenty of everything – especially football – I loved the game. I would travel to matches. My dream was to be a footballer. I had several trials with local clubs, but that was all. I was very disappointed. It made me think of returning to Jamaica.'

As the years rolled by, things steadily grew worse at home. Barrington felt very isolated from the rest of the family; at times it was like being a lodger.

'I was not close to anyone . . . I just existed . . . we lived in a mid-terrace, which had three bedrooms for ten of us . . . more problems followed . . . my parents divorced . . . my mother died the year I became British Indoor Champion . . . although we were not very close, I had nothing but pity for her.'

Secondary school years were a nightmare!

'I had a racist fight on the first day. I was the only black kid in the class. After a few fights no one called me names! Nearly every boy in the class got thumped – my older brother helped out, as well.

'Probably, my old school was glad to see the back of me! I did eventually calm down a little, which is why they made me a prefect, I suppose. I think the other kids knew that I had a less than ideal family life.

'Of course, I was the fittest kid in my year, but I was small for my age, which worried a lot of people. I had to wait until I was twenty before I grew close to my present height. Shaving, that all-important rite of passage into adulthood, was to follow a few years later! Illness and traumas suffered as a child may have caused my lack of growth. Everything seemed to be happening in slow motion; I felt a freak. My brothers were all big, strong and taller than I was, even at the age of twelve. As far as height was concerned, I did not appear to be from the same family as my siblings.'

It was, obviously, no accident that Barrington peaked in athletics at the age of thirty-eight. Before she died, Barrington's mother told him that at his birth she'd noticed that he was rather different to the rest of the family.

While at school, he belonged to the army cadets for a few years. He even considered joining the army but it was really only to escape a desperately unhappy home. A racist fight was the reason Barrington left the cadets. He had been blamed for it, although others in the unit had started it.

The love of guns, which had begun while a cadet, did not leave him until God took that and other things away, eventually replacing bad desires with much more wholesome interests.

His first job, after leaving school, with four O-levels, was in a factory. It was rough and tough! An incident, one day, led to him being threatened with having his throat cut! Barrington was so unhappy at home, he wasn't bothered if he died – to him death could be no worse than life, or so he felt just then.

Football was like a god to him but because he was so small he failed to make the grade.

It was another blow.

Violence seemed to haunt Barrington from his early school days.

A so-called 'friend' from school turned a twelve-bore shotgun on him once, while they were out shooting. He was made to crawl and beg for his life.

'My friend was a notorious criminal from the age of eleven. We had a fight one Saturday and he was simply getting his own back . . . I pleaded with him not to shoot me, as he pressed the shotgun against my temple, and swore at me . . . and more . . . it shook me up pretty badly . . .'

The incident which finally drove him to seek help at church, involved a mate of his who was related to the Tongan royal family. His friend's uncle, who had been a heavyweight boxer, had just been shot in Chesterfield.

' My friend was a big bully – he must have fallen out with me after I stopped him beating up a Chinese lad . . . my crazy friend tried to take my head off with a Japanese sword in his own uncle's house. I believe I received my sprinting speed that day! I escaped from the house and never went back!'

Barrington's sister had returned home from Nigeria. Death was really occupying his mind, so she suggested that he should go to church. Having nothing else to do, he went along. At the end of the meeting, one man asked him to come back another time. He promised and, as he never liked to tell lies, he returned. In fact, for the first time in his life, he had found somebody interested in him. At school he had been very shy, but this man had brought him out of himself.

On one occasion a Yorkshireman came to the church to preach.

'He explained about the love of God, who sent Christ into the world to die for my sins. I had never experienced love in my family, which by this time had broken up. And anyway, I had always been too "big" to show individual love to any one member. The preacher explained how Christ wanted to come into my life, which at that time was very unhappy and sad. He spoke about heaven and hell. I knew I wanted the love of God and wanted to go to heaven one day.

'For some reason, the message went right to my heart. It was as though nobody else was in that little church except me. I felt that God was speaking only to me.

'I looked around and nobody else seemed to be affected.

'I felt very uncomfortable.

'I realised that I had done wrong in my life, though I had never murdered or stolen anything.

'That night, believing Christ had died paying the penalty for my sin, I asked Christ – who had risen from the dead – to come and live in my life. It was tough at first, but slowly I got stronger as a Christian, as I read the Bible and prayed day by day.'

Barrington left full-time employment to return to further his education at Sheffield University. Having just become a surveyor, Barrington soon found that he had a bit of spare time on his hands in the evenings. With nothing better to do, he decided to go down to the Sheffield stadium for an evening's relaxation. A little crowd gathered as he long-jumped into the sandpit. He didn't mind, but instead kept thundering down the track before launching himself into the air, landing triumphantly in the sand. Everyone still kept watching. He thought he must have been doing something wrong.

'What club do you belong to?' asked one couple.

'None,' Barrington answered honestly.

Watching him were John and Sheila Sherwood, Olympic athletes, who assured him that he, without practice, was jumping further than anyone in Great Britain!

Needless to say, he was encouraged to join an athletics club in Sheffield in 1970. He was soon being put into all types of club events and usually won.

'This unorthodox athlete is undeterred by circumstances that would put off other erstwhile champions.' A newspaper reported:

'Ace sprinter Barrington Williams got Sheffield AC away to a flying start . . . The thirty-year-old local government official, from the Chesterfield area, not only scored a remarkable hat trick of individual victories, but he also pulled out an astonishing last leg of the sprint relay to give Sheffield the edge in the match' (The Star, May 12, 1986).

He almost missed the match because . . .' Amazingly Williams competed in a pair of borrowed spikes after inadvertently locking his own running shoes – and his car keys – in his car! Yet Rob Betts' size 9 ½s did a great job for him, as the Sheffield star won the 100, 200 metres and the long jump, in between watching the FA cup final on a portable television set in the pavilion!' He missed out on his warm-up because Liverpool had scored!

Barrington won the British Indoor long jump Championship at thirty-one years of age and was once ranked No.1 in the Commonwealth and 11th in the World Indoor Championships. Other achievements include: GB long jump record holder, 8.05 metres, 1989, RAF Cosford; British Indoor Champion, long jump, 1987, 1994, 1995; British Outdoor Champion, long jump, 1991, 1994, and World record holder for veterans 40+, 1996, Birmingham.His first international event was in Hungary (a communist country in those days), where they changed the long jump event from a Sunday to another day. Barrington has consistently refused to jump on Sundays believing that he should always put God first and keep Sunday for Him. Refusing to take part in

the 1988 Seoul Olympic long jump because of it being
held on a Sunday, he decided to sprint instead. A few
British Christian athletes, who were over there at the
time, formed a prayer group.

'I believe God put me in the British team for a reason,
and I have always sought to explain to fellow athletes
the good news of the Lord Jesus Christ.'

It was altogether a very exciting time to be in athletics, learning from the likes of Linford Christie, Daley
Thompson and Sebastian Coe.

As the oldest person in the British team at that time,
he rarely trained, ate whatever he wanted and didn't
take special vitamins, believing that God gave him the
strength to perform. He has regularly been drug tested
(twice one day), but Barrington explains the secret of his
strength:

'God has been very good to me, He has given me
strength to use my talent for Him.

'When Christ came into my life, I felt wanted, and full
of joy.'

Barrington was well aware that he wouldn't be able to
continue forever, but as he said, 'It is important to be fit,
but more important to be fit for heaven, and only Christ
can do that for us.'

For over eighteen years, Barrington has worked as a
building surveyor, or in a surveyor's office. In 1997, he
left to work part-time as he is doing more and more
coaching and charity work.

He is very 'up-front' with the subject of racism.

'I have had racial problems really since secondary
school. Racism has been bad in the working arena – as a
Christian and as a sporting personality. The situation
has been unbearable sometimes. But in spite of everything, I still thank God, for not giving me the easy
options in life. I have had to live life the hard way. I

finished my international career without sponsorship and working full-time.

'As far as colour is concerned, I believe that God is not interested in the colour of a person's skin but rather, what goes on inside the heart.'

10. THE TRAVELLER

Steve Bunn

Steve adjusted his seat belt. The aircraft was almost ready for its trans-Atlantic flight to Miami. Sitting next to him was Phil, his former colleague at the Midland Bank (now HSBC). Phil was already a seasoned traveller, having worked for six months on a kibbutz in Israel. On his return to England, Phil suggested that Steve might like to do the same, only this time the two of them would travel across the USA.

Steve was in his mid-twenties, had a steady girlfriend and a good career with the bank ahead of him. Somehow, inside of him, feelings were being stirred, leading him to conclude that there must be more to life than the Midland Bank (even though they were a good employer!) I don't suppose he will ever forget the day he handed in his notice.

'It was a big step for me. I knew I was chucking in my career, with no real plans for the future. It was all a bit risky.'

Steve and Phil managed to get a good deal with Freddie Laker's airline company. Their tickets were only fifty pounds each!

The flight was uneventful, apart from the usual tension preceding take-off and landing, interspersed with boredom, cramped limbs and attention from attractive flight attendants.

The US customs officer wanted to know how much money they had. Steve had saved about one thousand pounds.

'Ah reckon that'll last y' about one month!'

They thought so too.

Stepping on to American soil was a great feeling. At last, they were free from the daily grind back home and were heading for sunny California. Their plan was to travel by Greyhound bus, as it was cheap, and then to stay with friends on the West Coast.

Steve dumped his rucksack down on the seat in the bus station.

That was when he saw it.

It wasn't very big and there was only one. It was a little booklet. On the cover were the words, 'That you might have life.' Steve had no idea about its contents. It looked interesting. He picked it up, stuffed it in the bottom of his rucksack and, basically, forgot it was there.

The bus wound its way from Miami, through New Orleans, around the side of the Mexican border and eventually delivered its weary passengers at their destination in California.

The warmth of the welcome, given by their friends, was matched only by the weather. The days flew by. Near the end of their holiday, they travelled up through some mountains in the North and bumped into an American couple who owned a restaurant. They were so enamoured with Steve and Phil's English accents that they promptly offered the two men jobs as waiters! US customs allowed them to extend their stay so, for the best part of six months, they donned their waiters' outfits and served exceptionally fine food and drinks to diners who were similarly captivated by their accents.

As they had nowhere to live, Steve and Phil were allowed to make the extended garage into their home – the nearby river being their en-suite bathroom and laundry facilities. It all sounds pretty primitive but in California the weather is almost always perfect.

It was while doing this job that Steve eventually got round to emptying the contents of his rucksack; out fell the little booklet. (Steve wasn't perhaps in the best condition to read it as he happened to be stoned on cannabis.)

Anyway, read it he did! It took him a couple of hours. It was, in fact, a part of the Bible: John's gospel.

Steve can vividly remember the effect those few pages had on him at the time.

'They left me with a picture of Jesus that no one had ever shared with me before. I guess up until that point, if anyone had asked me who Jesus was, I would have replied that He was one of a number of great men who had something to say. However, John's gospel introduced me to the fact that Jesus Christ was there right at the beginning, before all the other men, because He was God's Son.'

This was all pretty mind-blowing stuff and knowing that he had read it stoned, the first thing he realised was that he had to read it 'straight'! Which is exactly what he did the very next day – again and again! Steve felt as though he was being cocooned over the following two weeks. He likened it to being on a journey that was leading him to come to a decision.

'Phil and I were walking towards the river and we had to cross a road. As I was halfway across, a car nearly hit us! I clearly heard (not audibly, but as an inner sort of prompting) "No, you're not ready for this yet, you still have a decision to make."'

Steve had literally come to a crossroads in his life. Now that he knew who Jesus was, he could go in either of two directions. He could ignore the truth and carry on as though nothing had changed or he could surrender his life entirely to Jesus Christ; this is what he did.

'Without a doubt, He fulfilled His promise that He would come into my life. With Jesus Christ on the "inside", over the next few days and weeks, a cleansing process began, which turned my world upside down.'

Steve's new relationship with the Creator God had come about, initially, by simply reading God's Word in the New Testament. No one had persuaded him; he had come face to face intellectually and emotionally with the written Word – the Bible and the living Word – Jesus Christ.

'It was as though everything in life had been a jigsaw puzzle with no picture, but on that day, the last piece had been put into place, completing the wonderful scene of the Creator and His creation back in communication.'

The restaurant owners were making plans to go to Seattle to start up another business during the closed season. Who would look after the restaurant in California? By now, they trusted Steve and Phil so much that they left them in charge for a couple of months!

'We had a total free rein over the place. We had our own bar and everything we wanted to eat. Phil thought it was a dream come true!'

Meanwhile, Christ was speaking to Steve about being 'cleaned up' in order that his relationship and communication with God could grow, in a way that would be meaningful. He still used marijuana for a number of days; but it became clear through crying himself to sleep that getting 'stoned' wasn't really helping him in this new love-relationship with God! There came a point where he handed everything over to God.

On a visit to a bookshop some weeks earlier, a book entitled *The Way* had caught his eye. At the time it had really intrigued him and it had stuck in his mind, so after becoming a Christian, Steve went back to the shop and purchased a copy. It was actually a full Bible, a translation of the Living Bible. He took it back to the 'garage-home' to read in the ensuing months. He still had not met another Christian.

Steve was a Bob Dylan fan! When he discovered that Dylan was doing a concert in San Francisco, Phil and he immediately made tracks to the theatre. As they had covered nearly three hundred miles, they booked in for two performances. After the second, everyone poured out on to the street. Outside, in the general mêlée of excited, loud and exuberant youth, perhaps under the influence of a variety of legal and illegal substances, Steve met a whole bunch of guys, who were really fired up about something. They seemed 'OK'. There was a lot of talk about 'the power of love' and 'how important it is that you don't sit back and do nothing in life'. Frankly, Steve found it all quite interesting. The guys belonged to some sort of camp, on the outskirts of San Francisco, to which they invited Steve and Phil for the weekend. Being their 'own bosses' and not having much else to do, they went along. Years later, Steve admitted, 'You might think it was a pretty naïve of us to go off with total strangers . . . it was! I don't recommend it!'

No one actually went about advertising who they were. There was no doubt however, that they were absolutely sold out on the work they were doing. It all sounded good. Compared with what others were, or more likely, were not doing, the outfit didn't appear too bad on the surface. Steve and Phil were constantly being told that they could change their world. It made them feel very guilty for not joining them. The teachers in the group seemed competent and professional, giving seminars and giving 'calls' for commitment and yet, despite the passion for their concepts and the dedication of the entire camp, Steve had a few questions of his own to ask them.

'For a start who do you say Jesus is?

'Is He the Creator - God?'

Steve had only been a Christian for a couple of weeks. He was not a member of a church. He had not attended a Bible college. He did not fully understand what had happened to him, but he did grasp from John's gospel that Jesus was the Son of God, the Creator and only Saviour who could forgive our sins. He had come to that conclusion, not only by reading about Jesus, but by his own personal experience. (When a person becomes a Christian, the Holy Spirit – the personal power of God at work in the world today – comes to live within that individual. The Holy Spirit is the Spirit of Truth. He gives discernment to His children when they are confronted with error, even to a young Christian like Steve.)

Steve had walked into the clutches of a cult: the Moonies.

Prayer was a new experience for Steve. He sure used it that weekend!

When it came to 'the crunch', the Moonies did not recognise Jesus for who He was and is.

Steve rumbled that all was not right, even though part of him wanted to stay, because of the positive teaching about love. The cult uses psychological manipulation to suck victims into the spiritually fatal clutches of error.

Making his escape, Steve left the city to return to the safety of friends. It was they who, on hearing of his experience, revealed the actual identity of his 'weekend friends'.

Horrified, Steve realised he must get Phil out of the camp. How could he have left his best mate in such a place?

So, with a six-pack of beer and a truck, they all drove back over the three hundred miles to San Francisco. They were only just in time. Such was the intense psychological pressure of the group, that Phil was within a hair's-breadth of joining the cult. Steve explained everything and, with Phil on board, they beat a hasty retreat back to the restaurant!

It was good to be back at work.

In any free time he could grab, Steve invariably wrote home to his girlfriend, Deb. Of course he had told her about what happened after reading the little book.

'I think it must have been pretty scary stuff for her, especially as she would have considered herself a Christian. We had had a long-standing, full relationship for eight years. It had always been my intention to go back and marry this girl, and even when I became a Christian, I prayed and prayed that God would sort things out. Things could have gone either way. I had established in my mind that regardless of where Deb's spiritual thoughts were, it was not a relationship I intended carrying on with.'

The only born-again Christian, whom Steve had met before was a guy from England who was working in Australia. Steve sent him a postcard telling him what had happened, asking if he had had a similar experience and to get in touch with him.

Steve had started his Bible reading at Genesis, three chapters a day, and by the time he had reached 2 Samuel, a postcard arrived from Australia. Brian was overwhelmed with joy, as he had been praying for Steve for a number of years. The card was littered with quotes from other parts of the Bible. Steve looked them all up, discovering extra encouragement from the New Testament.

'My best mate, Phil, couldn't understand what was going on in my life. He continued to get drunk and stoned, just as I had done. He would still say that "Christianity is just a phase you are going through and will come out the other side!" This "phase" has lasted for over twenty years! Phil hasn't, as yet, got my kind of faith but he's a great guy and I respect him very much.'

After a couple of months, Steve did seek out a church. His previous impressions of such places provoked feelings of alienation, kind but he thought he'd go to find out what was happening in his heart. It was Christmas time when he ventured down to the village church; about 30 or 40 people had gathered for the service. The pastor was overjoyed when he heard what had happened in Steve's life. He listened to the carols. He knew the tunes but not the words and it was strange understanding them for the first time as a believer.

Steve had a fabulous Christmas with God!

'I can't say I joined the church community, but I did enjoy my time with them and especially the pastor. He was really brilliant, even though he made it quite clear that, when I returned to England he advised me not to marry Deb unless she had a real commitment to God. I took it all in but . . . !'

Steve was still writing to Deb about all that was happening to him. One thing he didn't tell her was his date of return to England. He had already bought the ticket but wanted to surprise her. The day before, he went to his mailbox to see if there was a letter from Deb: there was.

She had written to tell him that she had become a Christian! She didn't know that her letter would be the last letter he would receive before leaving the States.

Deb worked for the civil service and had been on a course. One evening they had all been invited to go to a jazz club. She had ended up sitting next to a guy, who it turned out, was a Christian. He had gone out praying that he'd have an opportunity to talk to someone about Christ and share his faith. He was a musician, so naturally they talked about music. He explained that he also played an instrument at his church. At the mention of church, Deb opened up and shared what had happened to Steve.

'My boyfriend has had some sort of "experience" in the States – what on earth does it mean?'

The musician was only too pleased to explain that 'God so loved the world that He gave His one and only Son that whoever believes in Him should not perish but have everlasting life' (John 3:16). He also shared from the Bible that, 'If you confess with your mouth "Jesus is Lord," and believe in your heart that God raised Him from the dead you will be saved (Romans 10:9).

Deb understood, for the first time, that her wrongdoing was cutting her off from God. The situation was serious because that wrong had to be punished. The good news was that Jesus, out of love, paid the penalty by taking the punishment Himself by His death on the cross. By rising from the dead, Jesus proved He was God and would keep His Word... that 'to all who received Him, to those who believed in His Name, he gave the right to become children of God' (John 1:12).

Before the end of the evening, Deb went into the car park and quietly prayed, asking God's forgiveness and for Him to be her Saviour and the new boss of her life.

You can imagine how Steve felt as he read her words!

'It was incredible. I probably could have flown back without the plane,' jokes Steve.

Deb and Steve were married a few months later! They now have two children: Anna and Leah.

Steve reflects:

'Part of God's plan was obviously to separate us for a while, when we were living in a wrong relationship, sort us out and then put us back together again in a right relationship.

'We each have a distinctive story about how God touched us an individuals. What's really precious in my life is that He chose to use only His Word, the Bible. It is so powerful that it can take someone from nowhere into eternity – even a guy stoned on drugs!

'I really would like to meet the person who left the little booklet in the Greyhound bus station!'

To obtain a copy of the booklet please contact Steve at:

'REAL LIVES'
Paternoster Publishing,
PO Box 300,
Kingstown Broadway,
Carlisle, Cumbria,
CA3 0QS

11. THE ALCOHOLIC

Mike Mellor

London at night has a special 'buzz' about it. Sophistication and sleaze compete to satisfy the desires and longings of people searching for true happiness. Strolling through Covent Garden as it rubs shoulders with its infamous neighbour, Soho, you might bump into Mike Mellor, with his unmistakable, mischievous smile taking complete control of his unforgettable face.

Who would guess, looking at him, that this guy had really 'messed up his life big time'?

It all started long ago with the first drink. No problem, he thought as a young lad in his teens. Contrary to expert opinions, Mike contends that no one is born an alcoholic. It didn't happen suddenly; it was a gradual thing. Mike was in the newspaper business by day and at night out with the band – two jobs well known for drinking.

'Every lunchtime I would go to the pub,' recalls Mike.

'It attracted me and drew me. Looking back, I was the kind of person who wanted to live for kicks and was always looking for a high.'

As time went by things began to go a bit sour for Mike. Slowly, he became more and more of a heavy drinker. He had the kind of job where he could be anywhere at any time. At first it was an hour at the pub for lunch, then two, then three . . .

In the end he was going to work for one hour and spending the rest of the time drinking!

At night things were no better. Working with different bands at various gigs, there was always plenty of alcohol to be consumed. Booze was like water to him now. The female singer in the band attracted his attention. The relationship blossomed! Over time they settled down and had children. However, life for Mike was getting a little too crowded. 'Prioritise' was shouting at his mind and conscience as he continued to spend more and more time with his drinking friends than with his family.

Deep down, Mike knew that drink was getting hold of him. Day after day he would fall into his car, drive off somehow, not even knowing how he got home. He was a danger to himself and others. Eventually the police took his licence off him for drunken driving. Even his own newspaper printed the headline: 'Newspaper man three times over the limit.'

Then he started the really heavy stuff.

Musically, he and his wife went separate ways. Gwen was a singer, but Mike did more theatre work. Over the years they backed many so-called 'stars'. Day and night he knocked back the booze. Slowly cracks began to appear in his life; danger signs were appearing at home and work.

'I knew I was being a dreadful husband and father. My children's only experience of having a dad was hearing this dreadful noise came from the bathroom when I was being sick every day and night. I then began letting people down. All of today was being taken up by apologising for yesterday. Sometimes on theatre jobs, musicians on either side would prop me up. I knew all the signs were telling me that I was collapsing. Gwen suggested I join Alcoholics Anonymous. "But they will tell me to stop drinking," I protested. You see I loved the flavour of drink and the effect of being drunk. I loved being with drunkards – they were my kind of people. But I also would wake up in the morning thinking I'm doomed, that's it, I've had it.'

One morning, at the office, a desk was carried in and put right next to Mike's. A new job had been created at work. In walked a raw nineteen-year-old lad with a Bible, which he placed in front of his papers. His boss must have had a sense of humour, placing two such opposite characters in close proximity.

'I could see that there was something very genuine about his life – unlike mine. The first thing I noticed was that he had whites to his eyes!'

His colleague had certainly got Mike's attention. Not that he was religious, but there was just something (he didn't know what) different about him. 'I would come in the morning,' Mike says, looking back, 'get a twelve-inch ruler and prop up my chin! From time to time this other bloke would speak to me about Jesus Christ.

'What always sticks in my mind is that all sorts of strange people used to come into the office. One chap said he was an inventor; he was a Scotsman about five feet tall with a little beard; he was also an atheist. The Scotsman was having a discussion with the new lad.

'"There is no God," said the atheist.

'"Yes, there is!" piped up the other, "I know Jesus Christ is alive."

'I remember turning round to them saying, "Why don't you both belt up. You will never know there is no

God until you die – and you . . ." turning from one to the other, ". . . will never know there is a God until you die!"'

But slowly, bit by bit, Mike was hearing things about Jesus Christ. He didn't even realise he was taking them in. Paul was also editor of a magazine for the youth group in his church. He would say 'Mike, just check this for spelling and any mistakes for me will you please?'

'I remember a cartoon that caught my eye, it was a drawing of someone running to catch a departing bus – the point being that when Christ comes again, if we are unforgiven, it will be too late.' Somewhere into his brain came the thought, 'Hey, that's me!'

Often Mike would be picking up books in the office and find leaflets about Jesus. 'Even the name JESUS made me feel bad. I knew I was wrong you see. My life was closing in. I would wake up in the morning feeling doomed. I had only recently got my driving licence back from the police, but I carried on my reckless living and driving just as before.' One particular afternoon, following a three-day drinking spree, Mike fell into the car to drive home. He hit a car – but didn't stop. He hit another, but eventually made it safely home. Gwen was downstairs; actually it was her birthday. She was having a little tea party with the children, with her parents as guests.

The door burst open, Mike fell in and collapsed in a heap. The phone rang in the confusion of Mike's entrance. It was the police. They were on their way round. Gwen was unaware that her husband had had a crash.

One Saturday afternoon, not long after this disgraceful incident, he was in the office with the young lad at work. Stating the obvious, but in a caring way, he said 'Mike, you can't carry on like this, can you? You believe in God, don't you?'

Mike muttered something like, 'I suppose so. '

But something deep was going on in his heart that day; Mike will never forget it. 'I never denied that there was a God, but my mind was saying, "How can you know for sure?" I left the office and went into the little toilet (the only private place available). Right there, I, Mike Mellor, alcoholic, with completely messed-up life, got down on my knees and prayed, asking Jesus Christ to come into my life. I walked back into the office. The young man must have been dying to know what was going on in my heart, but I never said a word about what I'd prayed. I just left the office, got in the car and headed home. I broke down in tears of joy for I knew Christ was alive. Jesus Christ loved me and died for me. Even if I crashed the car now, I knew I was going to heaven.'

Gwen has never forgotten that day of 8th September 1979. Mike burst through the door as she was in the kitchen preparing tea. 'Everything is going to be different!' he exclaimed, his face glowing, 'I've become a Christian!'

Oh yes, she thought, I've heard all that before, but what did he mean by 'Christian'?

'Of course, we are Christians,' Gwen replied. 'We live in a Christian country,' and then carried on with the preparing the meal.

Mike explained to Gwen, as best he could, that he really knew that something wonderful had happened to him – the actual desire for drink had been taken from him.

After many years of total addiction to alcohol this was indeed some statement. It was evident to all, and especially Gwen, that Mike had a drink problem but he himself never acknowledged it. The tell-tale signs were obvious – the sick state his body was in, the drink/

driving incidents, the loss of his driving licence – but still he never would openly admit to having a problem. Now there he was, standing in front of his wife saying he was a changed man and that because he had asked Jesus to take control of his life, the desire to drink had gone!

Gwen thought he must have been dabbling in black magic or voodoo. At first, she was terrified. Later, she was more relaxed, as the greatest thing she had wanted was for him to stop drinking.

As the days and weeks passed by Gwen found she had a new husband! Gone were the urges to drink – in fact there were no withdrawal symptoms. Mike, still full of joy, continued to work at the newspaper office with the same people during the daytime but, at night, he was off playing his trombone in theatre shows. It was the talk of local musicians.

'What's happened to Mike Mellor?'

'He's got religion.'

'Bible-basher,' they taunted in Gwen's hearing.

One December night, after such a tirade from one member of the band in particular, Gwen told them, 'Well, I don't fully understand what has happened to him, but Jesus Christ has changed him completely.'

'Oh you'll be next Gwen,' said the drummer.

Gwen looked him in the eye saying firmly 'Oh no, not me!'

But the new Mike was definitely different. He showed great patience and love with Gwen as he pointed out a verse in the Bible to her. 'If anyone is in Christ he is a new creation, the old has gone, and the new has come' (2 Cor. 5:17). She could not deny the miraculous change in Mike. It was a 'power' too great for her to argue with. She battled within herself as she refused to admit that she, too, needed Christ in her life. On her way home in the car one night, she remembered some words from the

Bible from Sunday school, years before – 'Why have you denied me?' (the words of Jesus to the disciple Peter must before the crucifixion).

At last Gwen gave up the battle going on inside her and received Jesus Christ into her life. She asked Him to forgive all her sin and come into her life. She describes how she felt: 'I felt so clean, so happy. I was different. I was seeing everything in a new light. I had four lovely daughters – now I wanted to spend as much time as possible with them. I viewed my singing career in a different way. What was I actually singing? Were the places I went to, day after day, the right atmospheres to be in?'

Though her lifestyle began to change, the happiness she was experiencing, along with the fulfilment she enjoyed, was never to leave her.

So, how does Mike view his old habits?

'There is no cure for alcoholism. I know that is a controversial statement! It's like going into the garden and picking up a weed. You take the top off but the root is still there. What Christ did is pluck out the root. What God gave me that day, was such a clean, pure happiness that there was no competition with what I could get from drink. I am thankful that I got into a mess. To have gone through life on an even keel, being a nice chap, would have meant going to hell when I died. With hindsight, I am strangely thankful that this crisis arose in my life. It woke me up to ask, "What is life really about?" and "What lies ahead for me?" I feel that though bad things happen in life, it is often through those bad times that we find the meaning to the big questions of life.'

The bright lights and razzmatazz of London's theatre land have once more attracted Mike to find work among musicians and performers of Covent Garden. This time, however, he put aside his trombone and became full-time pastor of a church in the locality.

If you have a problem, an addiction, need advice and/or live in London and would like help, please contact:

Covent Garden Evangelical Church,
The Vine Christian Centre,
Nottingham Court,
Shorts Gardens,
London WC2

or: mgmellor@aol.com

12. THE ABUSED

Marie Joy

How does a person cope with life after being abused as a child? Marie Joy (not her real name) shares some of the intimate feelings of one who has had dark secrets in the shadows of her past. Her honest reflection does not concentrate on apportioning blame, which often leads to bitterness, but rather on how to rescue a life that has been damaged by another's wrongdoing.

'When I was born, a decision had to be made between saving my mum's life or mine; the doctors tried to save my mother.'

In all the confusion of the labour ward and the seriousness of the situation, it took some time for everyone to realise that the baby had, in fact, survived. Marie Joy was alive, but not without problems. During that time, her lungs were permanently damaged.

'From that day on, I seemed to have dysfunctional lungs. I spent the first few years of my life in and out of hospital, until one day I was moved to a children's convalescent home. I was sent there with other children who had heart or lung defects and those who couldn't carry on a "normal" life.'

She arrived with eleven other girls, who were put in one dormitory together. That group of twelve girls washed, worked, slept, played and ate together.

'When we did schooling we were in the same class. During the time I was there I watched all those eleven girls die, if not in front in me, they were very near. This left me with a real desertion complex. If I loved anyone or got close to anybody then they would leave or die.'

From that point on, Marie Joy didn't seem to fit into any age group. The 'powers that be' tried her with an older group, then a younger set. Still nothing seemed to work as well as being with those original eleven girls, who had been very much on her age level.

'The institution was a very austere, abusive place. The floors in the dormitory were concrete and it didn't have curtains. I remember that there was a wall halfway up . . . and wire netting was halfway up to the ceiling so that the air could come in (the theory being that we fight and become strong). If we misbehaved we were locked up a room that had bars and left there until "they" thought we had stopped being bad. This really meant until we had stopped crying.

'Our parents or guardians were allowed to visit us for one hour every fortnight if they could get there. Cars weren't readily available in those days, so it wasn't often that we saw our relatives. When we did, it was like visiting time in a prison – we sat at one side of a table and the visitors at the other. We were allowed to talk but not to pass things over, not allowed to touch or kiss. It was very cold and clinical. Although we knew we belonged to our parents, we didn't feel as if we did – it was a very strange feeling. It was as if we were on the outside, even though we were sitting with our own parents.

'Because there didn't seem to be people to keep an eye on us, we were very open to mistreatment. I remember once I cried after my dad had been to see me, so they locked me in a room and tied me to a bed. The room had bars on the windows and the door locked . . . and I think I was left there for days. I was made to drink my own urine and I was sexually abused in there.

'"They" said that until I stopped crying or showing emotion I wouldn't be allowed out. This happened on several occasions when some of us had been naughty and had been caught for misdemeanours. We were told never to speak about it or we would die too. Having seen our friends die, from whatever reason, it was very real to expect that we would be killed too.

'We lived in this fearful environment. We were fed and clothed. After showering, we stood in a circle and a nurse would come in with a big box of clothes and we would stand there until she threw something that would fit us, including vest, pants, jumper, skirt. To have no privacy made you feel very vulnerable. We had lockers but they were not private; there was nothing that was our own and if we gave any sign that we weren't happy with this then we were punished. The light punishment was to be sent to bed. The people who shared your room were not allowed to talk to you – it was called "sending you to Coventry". If someone was found talking to you, then they had to bear the same punishment as you. So we were not encouraged to talk about anything, let alone the injustices we felt had been done to us.'

Marie Joy became very angry and tried to escape. She only made it as far as the railway station. Her thinking was that if she boarded a train, it would take her home. When the police found her and returned her to the institution, she tried to talk to them about what was going on, but they did not believe her.

'I thought if they won't believe me, who will?'

With hindsight and with other instances of abuse coming to light only now, a full investigation should have been mounted. Unfortunately, legislation and public awareness was sadly lacking then. However, much has and is being done to tackle past injustices.

Marie Joy was forced to suffer these conditions for a few more years. 'Some of the people there, who were doing the abusing, were what I called "religious" people. I assumed that because of the clothes they wore. They did not behave like godly men and some of the abuse was very much from them.

'I was eventually allowed to go home but by this time I couldn't laugh or cry, I was emotionally locked up. My parents said I wouldn't even ask for a sweet and I was very strange to be with. This was because they told me if I did anything wrong I would be sent back. I was so in fear of being sent back that it was like "living on egg shells" all the time.

'I missed quite a lot of schooling. Although we were taught to write our names and addresses, we mostly copied things from the blackboard. We were told to write home every month; we had to put down what they said and everything was vetted. I could do that, but I couldn't read a book, understand it or write about it.'

After several months her parents realised that they couldn't do a thing with her. She had seemed to develop severe asthma at this point, so they took her to a priest, who they thought could help her.

'I went there once a week for several weeks. It was during these sessions that this priest raped me. That was the last straw, I would not trust another man. I would not trust God; I hated God.

'I hated men of God. I would not go into a church. The only thing I cried out was, "God if You are real, how did you let these people do these things to me, how do You let them do it to my friends in the 'home' and do nothing to get us out of this mess?" My heart and thinking were in turmoil. I couldn't feel any sense of love or care, it was as if part of me was frozen and cut off from everybody else.'

Marie Joy had to return to school, but she found she couldn't cope in the class for her age. She was then about thirteen or fourteen years of age – academically, she was more at the level of a four-year-old. She admits that she didn't seem to fit in there. 'I was supposed to leave at fifteen so I just used sit through the whole thing. I couldn't do games. I couldn't join in with a lot of things, so I was just like a sore thumb to the class. On my way home one day, I was attacked by a gang, beaten up and assaulted. I remember crawling home and almost wanting to die. The next day I couldn't get out of bed because I was in so much pain and I was rushed off to hospital and it was found that my left kidney had been damaged and was not working. They didn't know if that was due to some drugs that had been used on me as a child, because in the "home" we were experimented on like guinea pigs to see if certain drugs would work in certain situations, or whether it was from the beating. The consultant said the right thing to do was to remove the kidney, but didn't think my lungs were strong enough to take the anaesthetic. On the other hand, if he left it in, I would be dead in three months because it would poison my whole system!

'Some choice!

'So, putting on a brave face, pretending I was somebody I was not, I said that he might as well have a go as I had nothing to lose.

'Inside I was absolutely terrified. I remember being in the hospital bed, in a big ward like a Nightingale ward, with all adults round me, thinking:

"What happens if I die?" and

"Where will I go?" and

"Will I ever know what normal life is to be with a family and to be loved?"

"Will I ever know what love is?"

"Will I always be ostracised?"

"Is there something different? Up to now, this has been a mess and I don't want to live any more like this, if there is something better."

'There were times when I literally shook with fear.'

During visiting time, a young man came to visit Marie Joy. Clutching a note in his hand, he said, 'In our school assembly we have been praying for you and I've come to give you this note before your operation tomorrow. If you would like, I'll come and visit you when you have had your operation.'

Looking back, Marie Joy feels that this was the first time she had seen such gentleness in a person.

'I just said "Yes, that's fine," and pretended that I could read the note – I couldn't! When the nurse came I asked her to read it to me.

'It said, "God says, you will live." I thought, "Fancy God sending me a letter!"'

Innocently, Marie Joy said to the nurse, 'How do I get to know God? ' The nurse replied, 'Oh, I don't know, but there is a Bible in the locker. I tell you what, I'll get it out for you. You open it up, put your finger in and wherever that is, I'll read what it says.'

Marie Joy thought to herself, 'God, if you are real and can help me, will you be real to me now.'

She put her finger somewhere in the Bible and the nurse read these words: 'Fear not, for I have redeemed (Marie Joy didn't know what that word meant!) you; I have called you by your name; you are Mine. When you pass through the waters, I will be with you; . . . When you walk through the fire, you shall not be burned; . . . since you were precious in My sight, you have been honoured, and I have loved you' (Is. 43:1-4).

'I can't explain to you in words what happened then, but I felt this overwhelming love of God hit me and I knew God was real. The God I had been blaming all these years for all these things, suddenly had all this love for me and I knew He was real. I felt like a little baby, wrapped in a pink blanket, covered in love. I didn't know what a lot of the words meant, but if He called me by name and He loved me and He thought I was precious, that was good enough to me!

'I remember saying, to this God I couldn't see, "I'll give you my life hook, line and sinker if you stay with me like this and don't leave me and help me through this operation." I didn't know any other language to use but I really meant what I said. I remember when I woke up after the operation, a little bit of me was disappointed because I thought I might have gone to this person, who loved me so much.'

The young man, who had brought the note, was as good as his word. He visited Marie Joy twice a week for about three months until she recovered. Not only did he read verses from the Bible to her until she learned them, as she couldn't read properly or write them down, but he also helped her develop those very skills, which she was lacking.

'During that time in hospital I felt God saying to me, "Marie Joy, I want you to nurse." I thought, "Here I am, fighting for my life, I am physically sick and not even educated and He asks me to nurse!" I was putting up this battle but inside I knew that God wanted me to nurse. I said, "All right, if you make me better and help me go to school and learn, I will nurse!"

'This was the beginning of my walk with God and my understanding of how to overcome fear. A lot of the things that had been done to me were evil and fearful but now I had met a God, Who overcame those very fears I had. In time He led me to a headmaster who got me on a pre-nursing course. There were 30 places and 100 people after them. The day I went for the exam my daily reading, in the Bible, was about the prodigal son. The first question on the English paper was, "Write the story of the prodigal son!"

'I couldn't believe it.

'I thought this must be from God, as I had only just read the story at home. There was a maths paper that I failed, but they decided to take me on if I did a lot of homework to catch up before starting the course in September!

'I started with girls, who were four years younger than I, going to do O-levels. Here I was sixteen, with these twelve-year-old girls. We were together for three years while we did this course.'

At this point, Marie Joy was still ill at times, but she was determined to get through the course. At the end of the three years, she had four O-levels and completed a pre-nursing course. 'It was my effort to go towards what God was calling me to be.' She applied for nursing at three hospitals and all three turned her down, because of her physical state. Marie Joy never gave up!

'I really felt God prompting me to try again at one particular hospital. I explained why I wanted to nurse and asked if they would they give me a trial, to see if I could do it. Years later, I found in my notes, a letter from my general practitioner. In it he said, "All that is keeping this girl going is a fighting spirit; if you turn her down, she won't have a go at anything else; just give her a try and she will learn in three months and have to pack it in anyway."

'Four years later I completed my training and loved nursing. God helped me through. I am still doing that to this day.'

Deep inside there were hurts Marie Joy had never faced and talked about. She had never talked to anyone about what had happened in the 'home' and how horrible it was. Somehow she still thought that if she spoke about it, they would send her back even when she was older.

'I tried to pretend it wasn't there. The only person I talked to about it, was Jesus.'

At the church, which she was attending, there was a new pastor. He and his wife were eventually able to discuss her past with her, helping her to deal with those fears that were crippling her inside. Together, they were able to work things through, with God's help. Having felt a victim all her life, Marie Joy understood that God wanted and was able to put the victim back on her feet again.

'I have to say that it took about a year, but slowly I became freer inside.

'As I walked along this road, I had to learn a very important thing called forgiveness. I had to learn that if I was to follow Jesus then I had to choose to forgive the people who had done these things. I thought they didn't deserve forgiveness. But God forgave me my sin and He wanted me to forgive them – to hand these people over by name to Him and trust Him to deal with them. I had to trust Him to sort it out so that I wasn't carrying this pain and bitterness and resentment inside me. As I chose to forgive them one by one, name by name, for the things they had done to me, I handed everyone over to this God I had come to know. I trusted Him to deal with it rightly and then I let it go. Then the pastor and his wife prayed for me that the healing of God would come to my own emotions and let me become free inside, as God had intended me to be free from the beginning of time.

'All those pains, hang-ups, resentments and bitterness, all that feeling of imprisonment and being locked up and always on the outside of the group because I was different, just seemed to drop off bit by bit. As God filled me with His love and healing, I no longer dwelt on the memory of those things. I no longer woke up with nightmares imagining me with a knife in my hand going to kill the person that abused me. All that was released from me. The God, who had saved me and who now was saving my emotions and memory from living in an imprisoned life, had set me free. The Bible says, "Then you will know the truth and the truth will set you free" (John 8:32).

Marie Joy could trust Him to care for, look after and protect her so that she could become the person He intended her to be, when He spoke to her the day she was saved.

She learned how to laugh and to cry, to begin to trust and build friendships and relationships – things that she would never have dared do before. 'Here I was alive and free to be me. Not only that, God started sending people to me who had been through similar things. He chose me to talk to them and listen to their pain and show the healing to them that He had given to me. What the devil robbed of me in my earlier years is nothing in comparison with all the love, freedom and joy Jesus has given me since.

'There were difficulties in my relationship with my parents because I was horrible teenager – very bitter. I blamed them and our relationship wasn't very good. What I did not know, at that time, was that they had been given no choice in letting me go to the "home". They had been told that if I died at home they would be

had up for neglect, which was the law at the time. I
didn't know that as a teenager, and blamed them for
sending me to a priest to get help and ending up worse
off than before.

'I began to love them, and our relationship was
rebuilt. I thought I'd never have a close mum and dad
and God gave them to me. In the last three years I have
been honoured and privileged to nurse them both
through cancer at home and let them die in peace, without any guilt.

'I thank God that he made the impossible, possible
and He turned the most horrible situation right round.'

P.S. Yes, Marie Joy's husband is the kind, gentle young
man who brought her the note in hospital: the man who
prayed, cared and loved her. As she says with a wry
smile on her face, 'Well, wouldn't you marry him?'

13. THE AUTHOR

Dorothy Carswell

'To the Manor born' – but without the title deeds! Some years ago, the popular television programme, of the same name, featuring Penelope Keith, began with shots of a magnificent country house. In real life it is actually part of the beautiful estate at Cricket St Thomas, Somerset. At one time, it was a wildlife park and is now a hotel, but when I knew it, it was in private hands. Unoccupied, the house and the estate, including the farms and sawmill, were supervised by an estate manager.

My family arrived in the early 1960s to take up residence on the estate in a semi-detached stone cottage, delightfully named 'Hollowells'. Nestling under a bank by a meadow, its typically English cottage garden neatly spread itself down to the small, winding river which bubbled on its way through a copse.

We had just moved from Cerne Abbas in Dorset, where my father had been the head gardener to the Digby family. Lord Digby was the Lord Lieutenant of the county. His daughter was Pamela Harriman, who after a colourful life, went on to be American ambassador to Paris. Lord Digby was highly honoured when he received the Order of the Garter from the Queen. Many eminent persons visited the manor house, including Sir Winston Churchill's grandson.

I had just passed my 11-plus entrance examination to the grammar school. I was beginning to grapple with Latin tenses, Shakespearian sonnets and the periodic table in chemistry when two things happened that were to change my life.

A new baby had arrived in the family. I loved to see the tiny clothes hanging on the line with the nappies flapping in the wind beneath the old apple tree. I felt so proud to take my baby sister around the village in the big pram.

But slowly it dawned on me that all was not well. Overhearing two ladies one day, I caught a snatch of conversation . . . 'she won't live very long, you know . . .' They were talking about my sister Barbara.

Gradually, I learned that my sister had Down's Syndrome. We had no idea what it was and had never met anyone with it. The family was advised to 'just put her away' in a residential home for the handicapped. In those days, there was not much else to do. But my parents decided to keep her at home and, with the utmost love and care, they devoted their lives to her. Daily they exercised her limbs enabling her eventually to walk. None of us really knew what lay ahead but we just got on with life.

Another baby arrived two years later – this time a boy. The labour was so difficult that my mother was taken into hospital. John was 'blue' at first, due to lack of oxygen when he was born, but otherwise everything seemed all right. Now, complete with a family of three children, my father decided to change jobs, moving to Cricket St Thomas.

We grew our own food, collected milk straight from the churn, had no 'bin men' and had freshly baked bread and good, home-grown vegetables. There was no pollution so the air was fresh and sweet smelling (away from the cows!). We had the 'run' of the place as no one was in residence. Acres of lawns, magnolia trees, cascading waterfalls and copses galore, were nature's playgrounds for me as a child.

One day I accidentally dropped a tray on the floor right beside my brother's pram. Like in a scene out of the film, *Mr Holland's Opus*, I called out to my mother.

'Mum, John never heard the tray drop!' We quickly began dropping all sorts of things behind him. We clapped our hands . . . no response. John was deaf.

Subsequent visits to the doctor and the hospital at Musgrove Park, Taunton, confirmed the diagnosis: John had no hearing at all. His syndrome, named Klippel-Feil, also included his top two vertebrae being joined together. In the sixties, sign language was discouraged and lip reading was the only thing allowed. (In fact I only learned British Sign Language when John was in his thirties.)

Now a teenager, I was beginning to experience, first hand, some of the surprises life throws at us. I never blamed God. I had occasionally attended Sunday school. I could see the hand of God all around me in nature. Probably there was a heaven; I didn't really know. I thought I wasn't too bad and therefore I was likely to go there . . . maybe.

The journey to school in Ilminster, was a long one. The first mile was by bike or on foot, which gave me plenty of time to think! Leaving my bike in a hedge until home-time (can you imagine doing that these days!) I then caught the school bus for the rest of the journey. This was when I caught up with my homework or got into trouble with the prefects for messing about. Although I wasn't to spend many years at Ilminster Grammar

School for Girls, it was a happy time. My friends, Caroline and Sally, helped me settle in, making the time more enjoyable.

Another classmate, Priscilla, invited me to a barbecue one weekend. Believe me, in those days there wasn't much going on, apart from the occasional Young Farmers' 'do's,' so I was glad to go. Transport was always a problem as we all lived so far from each other; mostly we relied on people to give us lifts. Those organising the barbecue had even thought of that, so my parents where happy to let me go. I had a great time. There were loads of young people. The food was good and everyone seemed very friendly. There was something different about them, though. I don't mean in an odd way, but being around these people definitely made me want to be like them. I discovered they were Christians. They came from different churches but mostly got together at a Methodist church. From then on I became a regular. I even went, sometimes, to the Baptist Chapel in Chard. It was when I began hearing and learning about Jesus Christ, who He was and what He had done for us, that I began thinking about what I believed.

I knew I was not like my new friends. They had something or Someone in their lives that I hadn't. I tried praying, but somehow my prayers didn't seem to reach further than the ceiling. I even tried to read the Bible and although I could identify with parts of the Psalms, the rest of it was incomprehensible.

A trip to London was organised by the youth group. I had never been so far in my life. This was the era of the Beatles, Mary Quant – the swinging sixties. I couldn't wait to see Carnaby Street, the Kings Road, Chelsea, plus all the other more usual famous sights.

I was only interested in the tourist side of things but we had actually gone to hear a well-known American evangelist, Billy Graham, who was at Earls Court. It was the year Cliff Richard publicly announced his faith.

Hundreds gathered in the arena and it was great to be there. I don't remember much of what was said but I did begin to wonder, 'If I died tonight how would I be able to face God?' I thought of all those times I'd argued with my parents. No, I was not guilty of murder but I could be accused of unkindness. Really, I had totally left God out of my life – but I didn't want to stay that way. At those big meetings, it was the custom for those who wanted to become Christians and to show they really meant it, to come forward publicly and stand at the front for a few moments, before being given helpful literature, a part of the Bible and someone to talk to. That was a bit too much for me, as no one in my part of the huge hall moved and I didn't want to be the first! Then it was all over and we were on our way home.

I felt unhappy inside because that night the penny had dropped, so to speak. I had understood for the first time that I was what the Bible called a sinner – someone who had done wrong. My wrong meant I could not enter heaven as it was where God was and He was perfect. Jesus Christ, God's Son had bridged the gap between heaven and me by dying on the cross, taking on Himself the punishment for my sins, which I deserved. He didn't stay dead but proved that He could give eternal life by rising from the dead Himself. To all who will receive Him into their lives He gives the power to become the Sons of God even to those who believe on His Name.

The next Sunday, at the youth group, I told someone I wanted to be a real Christian. In a small, back room of a church, on June 12, 1966, I bowed my head in prayer, asking God to forgive me. I thanked Him for dying for my sins on the cross. I believed He rose again from the dead and I received Him into my life as my own Saviour and Lord. Relief absolutely flooded my whole being. A few tears of joy were shed. It was like a huge burden being lifted. I don't think I looked any different – you'd have to ask my family that! But I did feel different on the inside. There was a real peace that is hard to describe unless you experience it for yourself. However, feelings come and go. My faith was not based on feelings; it was based on the indisputable fact of the resurrection. The Bible, once so difficult, became a delight to read. I had a desire to pray (now that I was in a right relationship with God it was thrilling to know that the barrier between Him and me had gone).

While all this inner change was going on in my life, my parents had to make some big decisions. My brother, John, had been attending a residential school for the deaf in Exeter since the age of three. Mum and Dad felt that it was the right time to move nearer to the school so that John could get home more often or even become a day-student. Dad found a job as gardener-handyman to a lady whose family owned hotels both in England and South Africa. We moved to Teignmouth, Devon, where my family spent many happy years. Barbara, my sister, could walk and was able to attend a special school. I decided that instead of going to university I would take up nursing as a career. I later married and had four children.

Becoming a Christian changed my life. Some thought it was just a phase I was going through . . . 'She'll get over it . . .' For over thirty years, God has kept me and daily given strength through His Word, the Bible, and prayer. Life is not without problems even for the Christian. Life continues to throw up surprises, including, in my case, a malignant skin cancer, which was successfully removed.

As God turns over the pages of my life and yours, who knows when and how the final chapter will be written, but when it comes to an end, for the Christian, it will say 'To be continued . . . in heaven.'

14. THE SAVIOUR

Jesus Christ

One criterion for being part of this book is to be alive.

Therefore, Jesus Christ qualifies.

The greatest man in history was a child refugee. Born into poverty and obscurity, as a youngster he was taken to Egypt to escape Herod and persecution by the oppressive regime of the Romans.

Jesus received no formal education, but rather, worked hard as a labourer. He never wrote a book or a song.

He formally preached and ministered for only three years.

He never spoke to flatter the authorities; He refused to compromise His message, and eventually was executed by crucifixion, at the age of thirty-three.

In those three years of public work, without travelling far, He made blind people see, dumb people speak, and deaf people hear. He healed lepers and lame people. He raised the dead to life. He fed thousands of hungry people with just a few loaves and fish. He instantly calmed a rough storm at sea and walked on the water, dispelling the fear of terrified fishermen.

Nobody spoke as Jesus did; He had authority.

He gave to the world the highest moral standard, preaching only what He practised.

Christ said, 'Love your enemies, do good to those who hate you, bless those who curse you, pray for those who ill-treat you,' and 'turn the other cheek' (Luke 6:27).

Jesus Christ gave dignity to women, respect to the disabled, significance to children, credibility to the family and status to each individual.

He has made an indelible impact upon our literature, art, music and architecture and is the foundation principle for our democratic freedoms.

Judas, who sold Him, cried, 'I have betrayed innocent blood' (Matt. 27:4).

Pilate, who ordered his execution, said, 'I find no fault in Him' (John 19:6).

John, the disciple, said, 'In Him is no sin.' The great missionary, Paul, said, 'He knew no sin.' And Peter said, 'He did no sin.'

It is impossible to fault Christ.

He had no sin, nor did any sin, because He was God manifest in the flesh (1 Tim. 3:16).

The Bible says of Jesus, that God 'became flesh and made His dwelling among us' (John 1:14).

Stripped naked, beaten and humiliated, Christ died on a cross. As He hung there, God laid on Jesus the sin of us all.

The Bible says, 'For God so loved the world that He gave His one and only Son, that whoever believes in Him shall not perish but have eternal life' (John 3:16).

'For Christ died for sins once for all, the righteous for the unrighteous, to bring you to God' (1 Pet. 3:18).

Jesus was punished in our place, that we might be forgiven for all our sin, all our wrongdoing.

Three days later, the tomb, where Jesus' body was laid, was empty; He had risen from the dead; He was alive.

Over an extended period of time, He showed Himself physically alive again to many people. He changed their lives, giving hope and peace to each one who trusted Him.

Jesus Christ had come to earth with a mission. He had come, not to call to Himself the righteous people, but sinners. He was more than a great example to us. He was greater than the supreme teacher.

He accomplished more than simply performing great miracles. The Bible states: 'The Father has sent his Son to be the *Saviour* of the world' (1 John 4:14).

Millions have followed Jesus simply because they trust and love Him. Civilisations have been changed as people have come to know God. He is able to set free each person who comes to Him. Instead of the hell we deserve, through forgiveness, God can reserve a place in heaven for us.

The Bible makes it clear that God's command to us, is that we turn from all that is wrong in our lives, and ask the once-crucified, now-risen, living Jesus to free us, forgive us and become our Lord and Saviour. When we turn our back on sin and trust Christ, He becomes our Saviour and Helper, making everything new. As our constant Companion He helps us in all the decision making of our lives. Jesus Christ has been such a real Friend to individuals for twenty centuries, all over the world.

Only Jesus had the power to defeat death and rise from the dead – He said, 'I am the Way, the Truth, and the Life. No one comes to the Father except through me' (John 14:6).

The stories in this book could only have been written if the life, death and resurrection of Jesus Christ were true. Real people have discovered Real Lives through Jesus Christ.

You can also experience the freedom and forgiveness of Christ. If you call out to Him in prayer, He will come to live in your life, giving you a relationship with God that will last through life, death, and into eternity. 'As many as received Him, to them he gave the right to become the children of God' (John 1:12).

You can discover this for yourself today.

If you would like more information about becoming a real Christian, please write to:

'Real Lives', c/o Paternoster Publishing,
PO Box 300,
Kingstown Broadway,
Carlisle, Cumbria,
CA3 OQS, England

or Email: carswell77@aol.com
or visit the web site: www.tell-me-more.org

Turning Points

Vaughan Roberts

ISBN 1-85078-336-5

Is there meaning to life?
Is human history a random process going nowhere?
Or is it under control – heading towards a goal, a
destination?
And what about my life? Where do I fit into the grand
scheme of things?

Vaughan Roberts addresses these questions and
others as he looks at what the Bible presents as the
'turning points' in history, from creation to the end
of the world.

This book does not read like a normal history book.
No mention is made of the great battles and
emperors. It will not help you pass exams or score
extra marks in a pub quiz. It aims to do something
far more important – to help you to see history as
God sees it, so that you might fit in with his plans
for the world.

OM
publishing

Why Me?

Roger Carswell

1-85078-133-8

'I thought this only happened to other people.'
'What have I done to deserve this?'
'Everything was fine, and then . . .'
'Why me?'

The problems and the experience of suffering provoke questions hard to answer. Why does it happen? What sense, if any, can we make of suffering? How do we cope with it?

In *Why Me?* Roger Carswell, author of eight books and widely travelled speaker, tells true life stories of people who have all experienced tragedy of one sort or another. Each one is a powerful and moving testimony to the hopes that can be found through knowing the God who suffered first.

**OM
publishing**

Journey to Murder
Road to Forgiveness

Jo Pollard with D.J. Carswell

1-85078-409-4

In the early morning light a bread van lumbered along the Hungarian road. The driver had no idea that his actions in the next few moments would later be reported by television and the media across the world.

The camper van parked by the roadside seemed innocent enough, but a distressed woman was trying to flag down the passing vehicle. Her eyes were badly swollen. Her face was battered as though it had been kicked by a football. She staggered towards the driver trying to push open her eyes, desperately trying to see out. As she approached the van she cried, 'I don't speak Hungarian, only English. I need the police – my husband is dead.'

Michael and Jo Pollard had spent thirty years delivering aid to Eastern Europe during their summer holidays. On the night of 4 August 1997, while sleeping in their camper van in Hungary, they were attacked, leaving Michael dead and Jo badly injured.

The ability to forgive in such terrible circumstances captured the imagination of press and public alike. Amidst personal suffering and grief, Jo had an inner peace. Her personal faith in the 'God who doesn't make mistakes' sustains and motivates her in the aftermath of that fateful night.

Journey to Murder is Jo Pollard's own inspiring account of this tragedy and of what lies behind her ability to forgive her husband's murderers.

paternoster Lifestyle